ORIGAMI
Hearts

by Francis Ow

Book design by Momoyo Nishimura

Published by Japan Publications Trading Co., Ltd.,
1-2-1, Sarugaku-cho, Chiyoda-ku, Tokyo, 101 Japan

First edition, First printing: January 1996

Distributors:
United States: Kodansha America, Inc., through Farrar, Straus & Giroux,
           19 Union Square West, New York, NY 10003.
Canada: Fitzhenry & Whiteside Ltd.,
           195 Allstate Parkway, Markham, Ontario L3R 4T8.
British Isles and European Continent: Premier Book Marketing Ltd.,
           1 Gower Street, London WC1E 6HA.
Australia and New Zealand: Bookwise International,
           54 Crittenden Road, Findon, South Australia 5023.
The Far East and Japan: Japan Publications Trading Co., Ltd.,
           1-2-1, Sarugaku-cho, Chiyoda-ku, Tokyo, 101 Japan

10 9 8 7 6 5 4 3 2 1

ISBN: 0-87040-957-3
Printed in Singapore

Acknowledgements

This book is not possible without the help of the many dedicated paperfolders, whom I am proud to have as friends.

David Petty, my regular correspondent in England and also an active member of the British Origami Society, has played a major role in this book, although only three of his models are included in this book, Petty has contributed by boosting my creative abilities, especially in times when I needed it most. Both he and his wife, Lilian, have supplied countless subjects relating to hearts. Models like "Baby Love", "Sweet Heart", "Love is Blind" and many others are the results of their brainstorming.

Paul Ee, my comrade, provided six of his excellent creations which I am proud to include in this book.

To the reat who have contributed, namely, Nick Robinson and Edwin Corrie of the British Origami Society, Francois Ziegler of France, Edwin Young of the U.S.A., Kunihiko Kasahara and Jun Maekawa of Japan, I offer my heartfelt thanks for all their excellent models.

My thanks to Eunice Lew of the U.S.A. for proofreading and for supplying diagrams of heart models by various paperfolders. My apologies for not including any, as some are similar, some too complicated and a few which I would like to include in this book but could not obtain permission from the creators.

I wish also to thank the Momotani family, Dokuotei Nakano of Japan and Vicent Palacios of Spain for their generous assistance.

I would especially like to extend my gratitude to Tomoko Fuse for introducing my works, not only to Japan but also to her publisher, Japan Publications Trading Co., Ltd., Tokyo, Japan.

My thanks to Yunosuke Murakami of Japan Publications Trading Co., Ltd. for his interest in my works and for publishing this book.

This book is dedicated to all my friens and all those mentioned here.

Francis M. Y. Ow.

LIST OF ILLUSTRATIONS

8

LI

Jewellery Box
ueda

Imperial Plaza 2F, 1-1-1, Uchisaiwai-cho, Chiyoda-ku, Tokyo
Tel. 03-3501-1441

6

7

9

10

11

12

13

13

uyeda
Jeweller

23

24

25

26

27

28

29

30

31

32

33

34

35

36

37

38

39

40

Contents

Introduction

This book is dedicated to matters of the heart and presented here are some ways in which this can be expressed through ORIGAMI, the Japanese Art of paper folding. I hope you may gain something from these pages, that the models presented here may be useful for you to convey your feelings to the one(s) you love and perhaps inspire you to creat your own models.

You can start folding from any part of this book as the models are not arranged in order of progressive complexity. However, certain models with the same starting bases are grouped together. In such cases, when you have difficulties in folding, simply refer to the models which appeared earlier.

Included in this book are also some modular folds. For these, you need to make the number of units required and then assemble them together. Cutting and the use of glue is not necessary and the only requirement is precision. Pay careful attention to the creases and location points and always look one step ahead. The diagram of each step is the result of folding of the previous.

Any type of paper can be used to fold most of the models presented here but for certain models, paper-backed foil is necessary. You can also use any color but red colored paper is most suitable for heart models. For models which show both sides of paper, "Duo-coloed" paper is preferred. I use standard Origami paper (150mm × 150mm or 6" × 6") for models which begin with squares. For models folded from rectangles, the proportions are cut from the standard square.

Use larger papers for practicing and when you are familiar with the folding procedures, fold it from a smaller paper. A smaller model not only looks more attractive than a larger one, it can also be easily contained in an envelope together with your love letters, cards or gifts. This will provide the recipient with a little something which is not easily available. Something meaningful, something origami coming straight from the heart.

As intended, most of the models here carry a hidden message, usually a massage of love. Some models are meant for just one purpose, some more than one. Some even for the purpose of insulting. For whatever purpose these are being use for, I hope you enjoy folding the models in this book. When you have folded all the models here, you will discover that like love, Origami is a many splendored thing.

Francis M. Y. Ow.

Symbols and Folding Techniques

- - - - - - - - - -	Vally line		Insert
— · — · · —	Mountain line		Fold to the front
————————	Edge of paper		Fold behind
— — — —	Crease line		Fold and unfold to crease
· · · · · · · · · · · · · ·	Imaginary line or X-ray view		Fold and fold
↘	Push in or sink		Pleat or crimp
↘	Enlargement		Turn over
⇒	Reduction		Turn to rotate
⇒	Stretch or pull	○ ●	Location points
↙	Repeat	└─┴─┘	Equal lengths

Division of 3rds

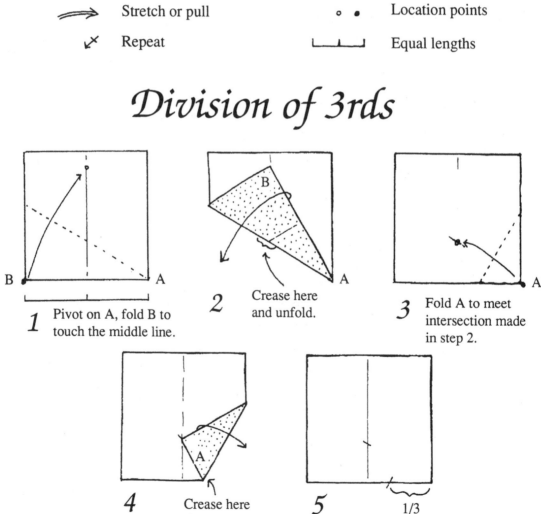

1 Pivot on A, fold B to touch the middle line.

2 Crease here and unfold.

3 Fold A to meet intersection made in step 2.

4 Crease here and unfold.

5 1/3

Heart Module 1

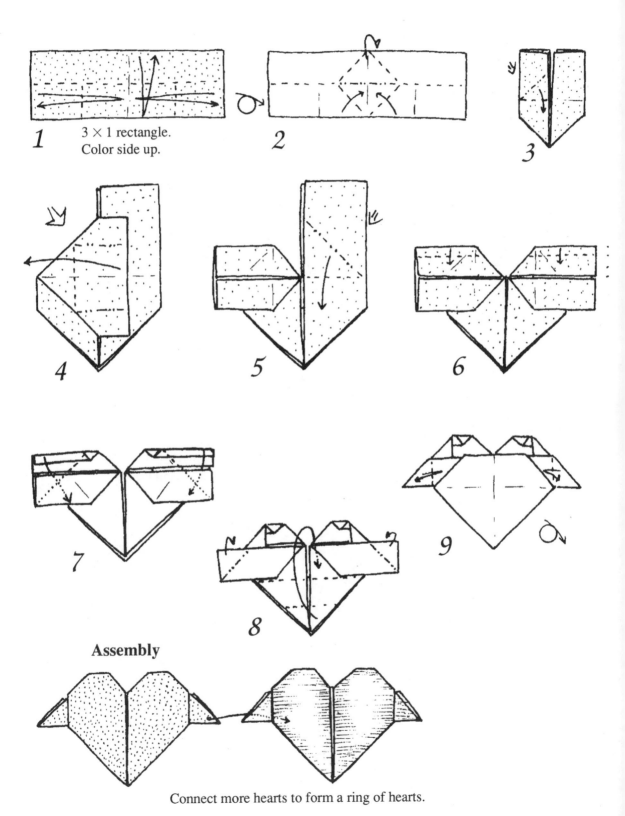

1 3 × 1 rectangle. Color side up.

2

3

4

5

6

7

8

9

Assembly

Connect more hearts to form a ring of hearts.

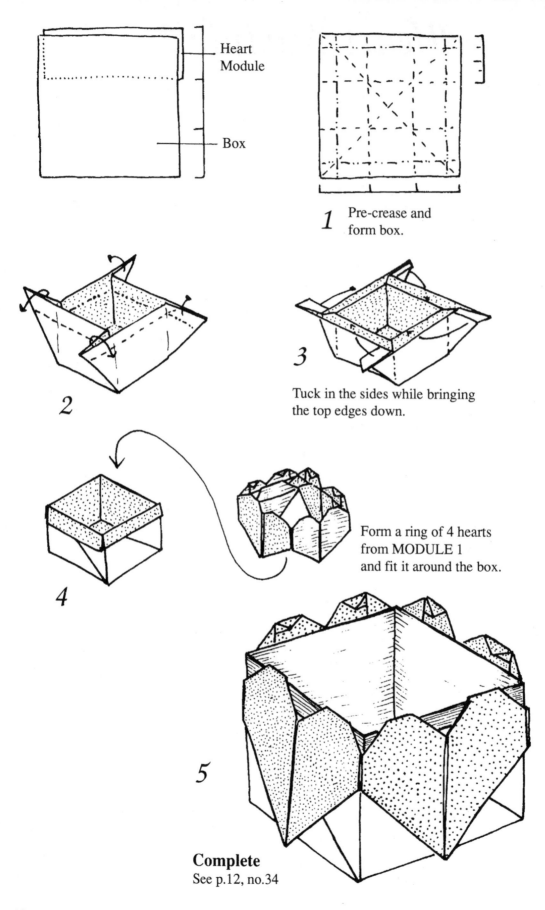

Heart Module

Box

1 Pre-crease and form box.

2

3 Tuck in the sides while bringing the top edges down.

4

Form a ring of 4 hearts from MODULE 1 and fit it around the box.

5

Complete
See p.12, no.34

18

Heart Module 2

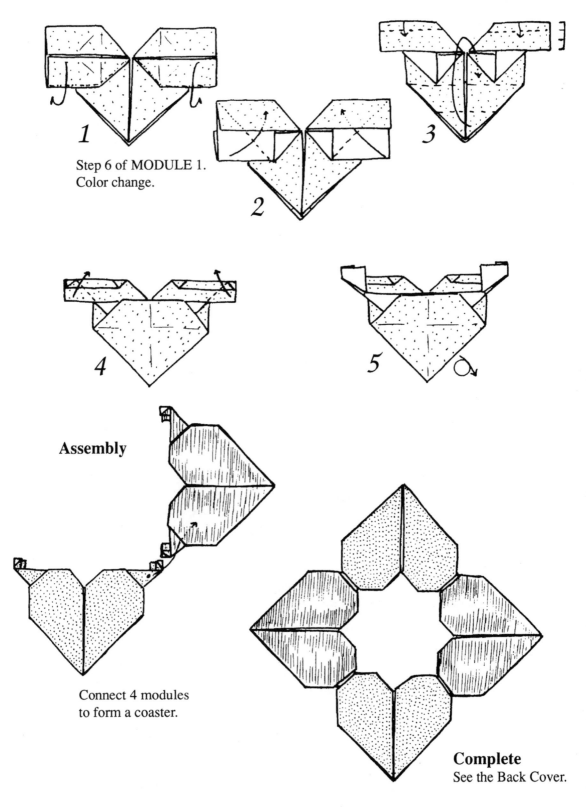

1

Step 6 of MODULE 1.
Color change.

2

3

4

5

Assembly

Connect 4 modules
to form a coaster.

Complete
See the Back Cover.

Heart Module 3

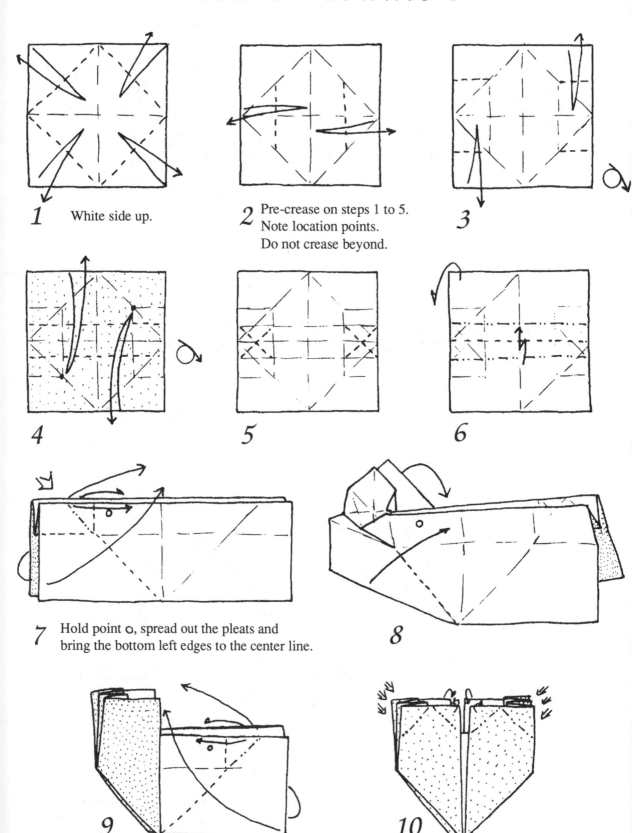

1 White side up.

2 Pre-crease on steps 1 to 5.
Note location points.
Do not crease beyond.

3

4

5

6

7 Hold point o, spread out the pleats and
bring the bottom left edges to the center line.

8

9

10

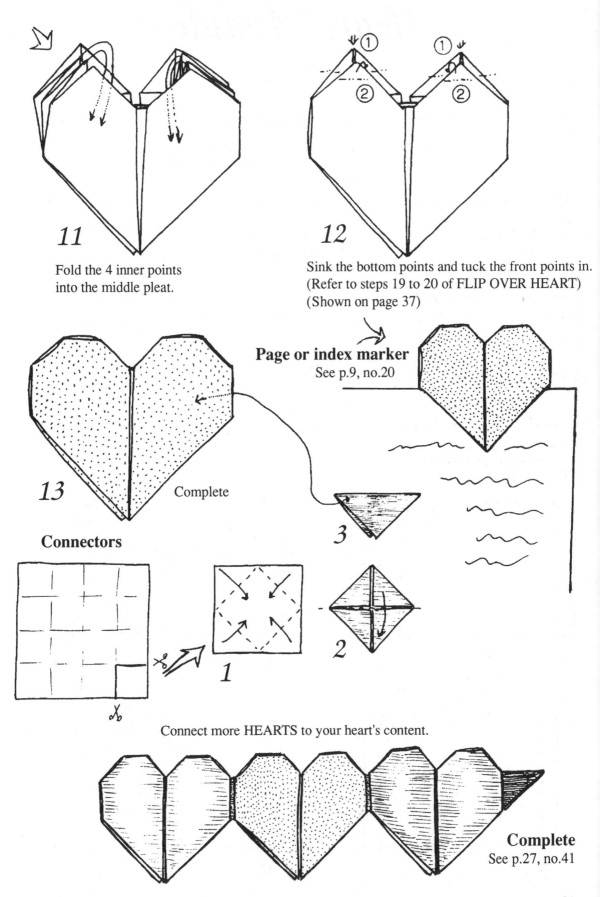

11

Fold the 4 inner points into the middle pleat.

12

Sink the bottom points and tuck the front points in. (Refer to steps 19 to 20 of FLIP OVER HEART) (Shown on page 37)

Page or index marker
See p.9, no.20

13   Complete

Connectors

1

2

3

Connect more HEARTS to your heart's content.

Complete
See p.27, no.41

Heart Module 4

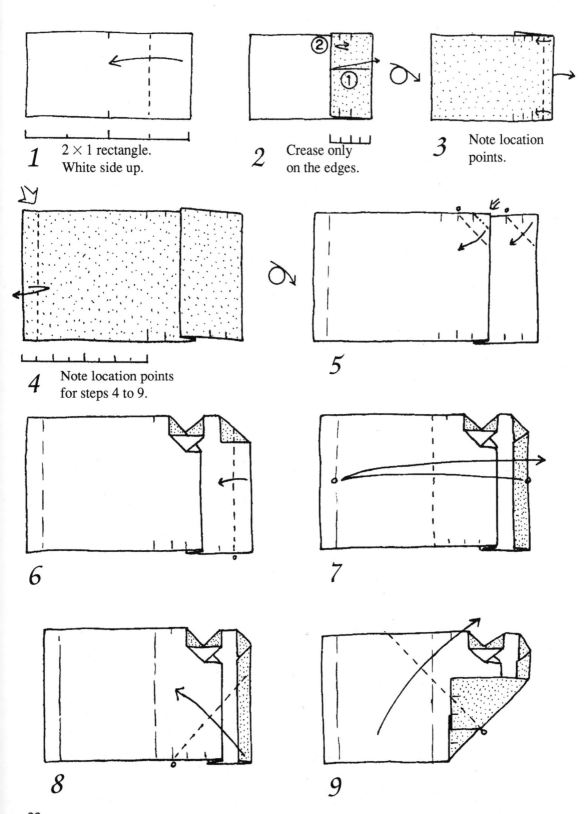

1 2 × 1 rectangle. White side up.

2 Crease only on the edges.

3 Note location points.

4 Note location points for steps 4 to 9.

5

6

7

8

9

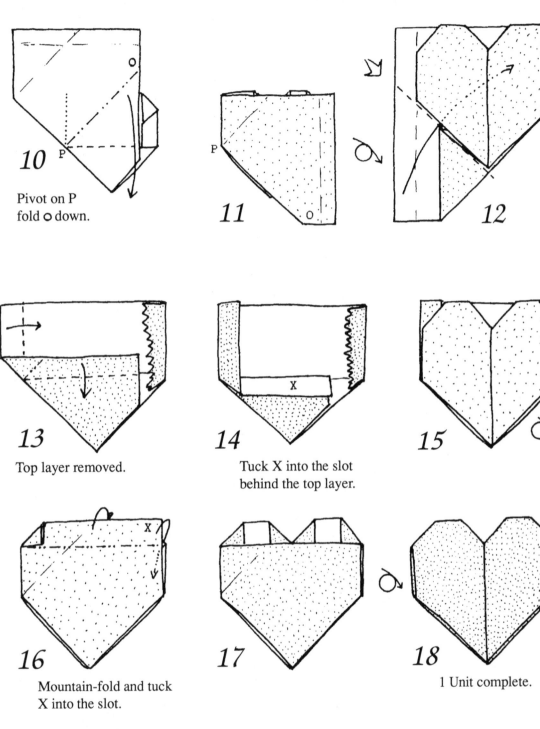

10 P

Pivot on P
fold o down.

11 P o

12

13

Top layer removed.

14 X

Tuck X into the slot
behind the top layer.

15

16

Mountain-fold and tuck
X into the slot.

17

18

1 Unit complete.

Connectors

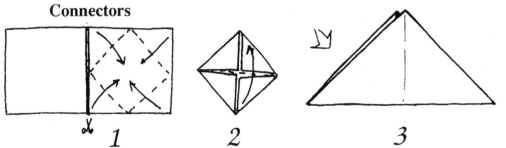

1

2

3

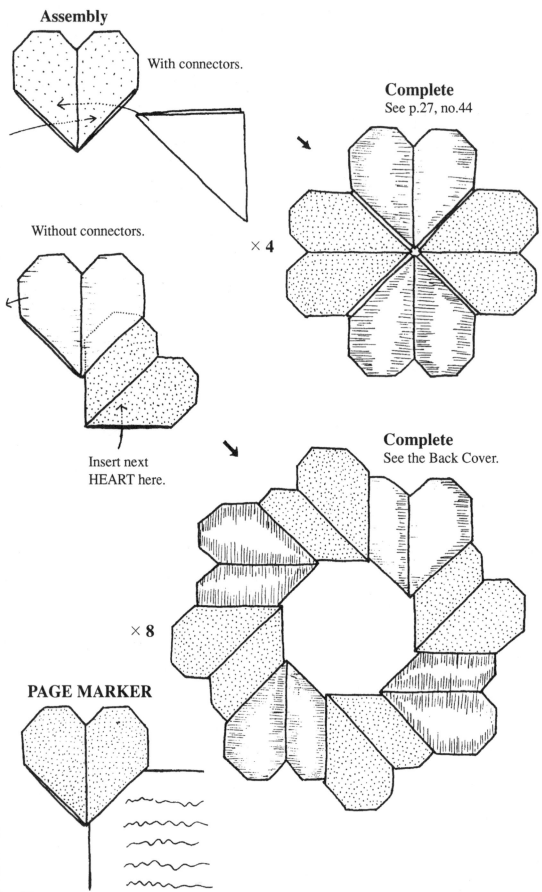

Assembly

With connectors.

Without connectors.

Insert next
HEART here.

× 4

Complete
See p.27, no.44

× 8

Complete
See the Back Cover.

PAGE MARKER

24

Heart Module 5

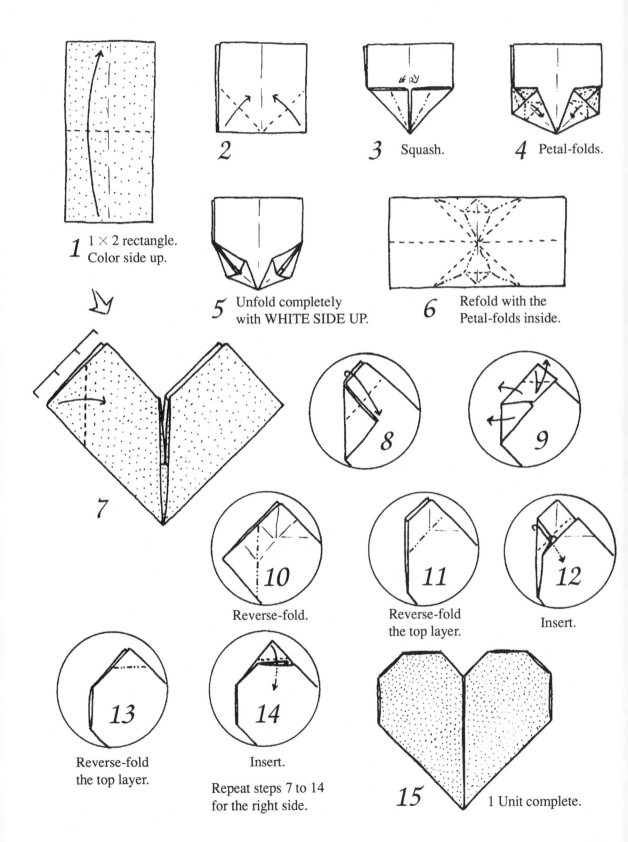

1 1 × 2 rectangle.
Color side up.

2

3 Squash.

4 Petal-folds.

5 Unfold completely
with WHITE SIDE UP.

6 Refold with the
Petal-folds inside.

7

8

9

10 Reverse-fold.

11 Reverse-fold
the top layer.

12 Insert.

13 Reverse-fold
the top layer.

14 Insert.

Repeat steps 7 to 14
for the right side.

15 1 Unit complete.

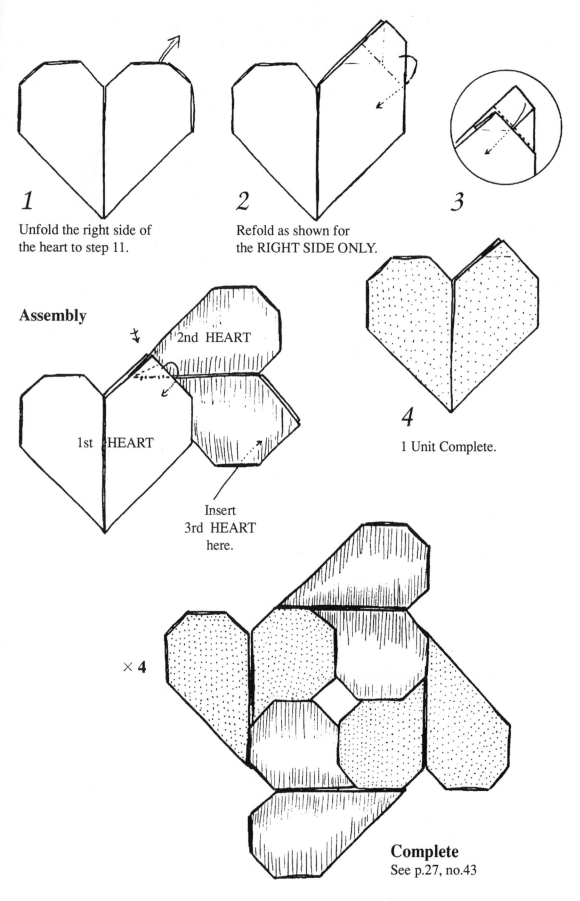

1

Unfold the right side of
the heart to step 11.

2

Refold as shown for
the RIGHT SIDE ONLY.

3

Assembly

2nd HEART

1st HEART

Insert
3rd HEART
here.

4

1 Unit Complete.

× **4**

Complete
See p.27, no.43

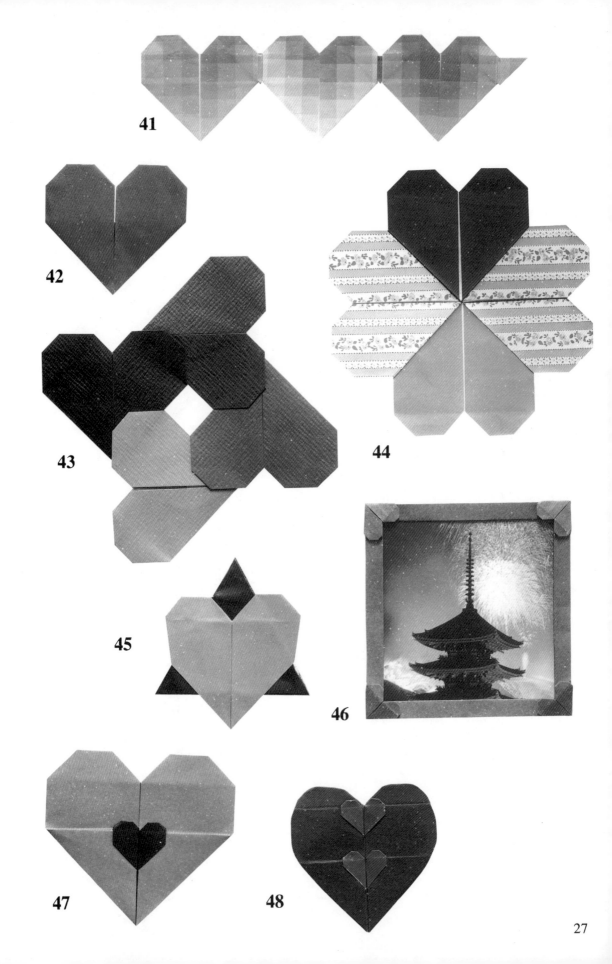

41

42

43

44

45

46

47

48

27

Heart-Cube Module

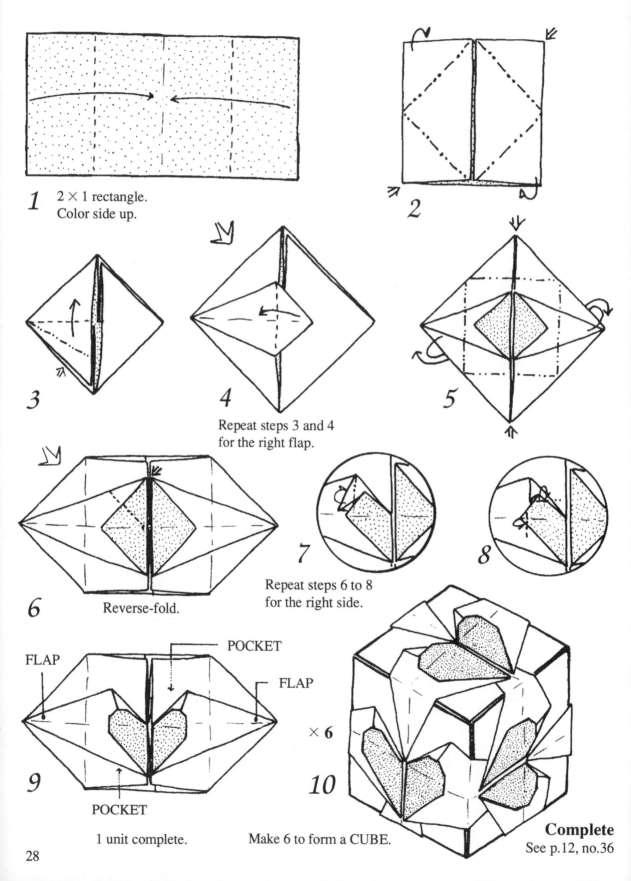

1 2×1 rectangle. Color side up.

2

3

4   Repeat steps 3 and 4 for the right flap.

5

6   Reverse-fold.

7

8

Repeat steps 6 to 8 for the right side.

9

FLAP

POCKET

FLAP

POCKET

1 unit complete.

10 $\times$ **6**

Make 6 to form a CUBE.

Complete
See p.12, no.36

28

Generations of Love

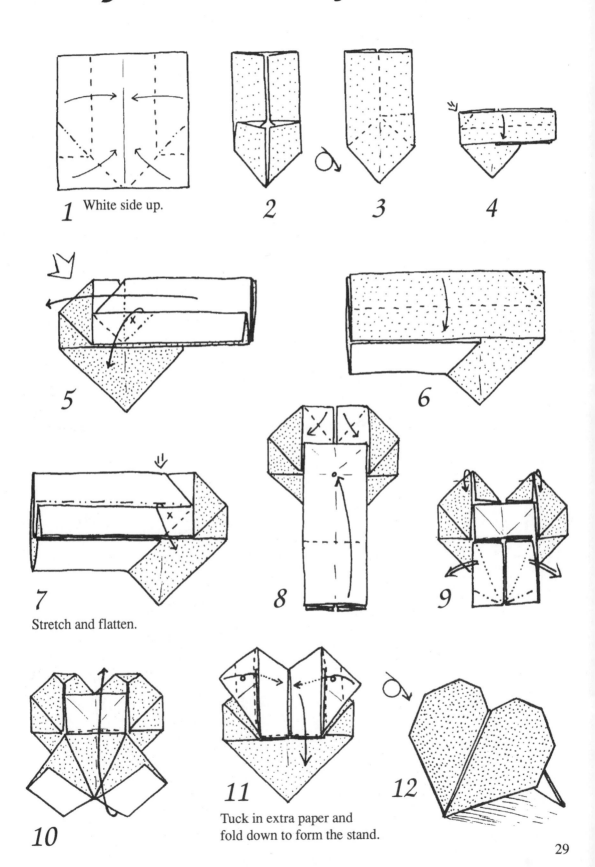

1 White side up.

2

3

4

5

6

7

Stretch and flatten.

8

9

10

11 Tuck in extra paper and fold down to form the stand.

12

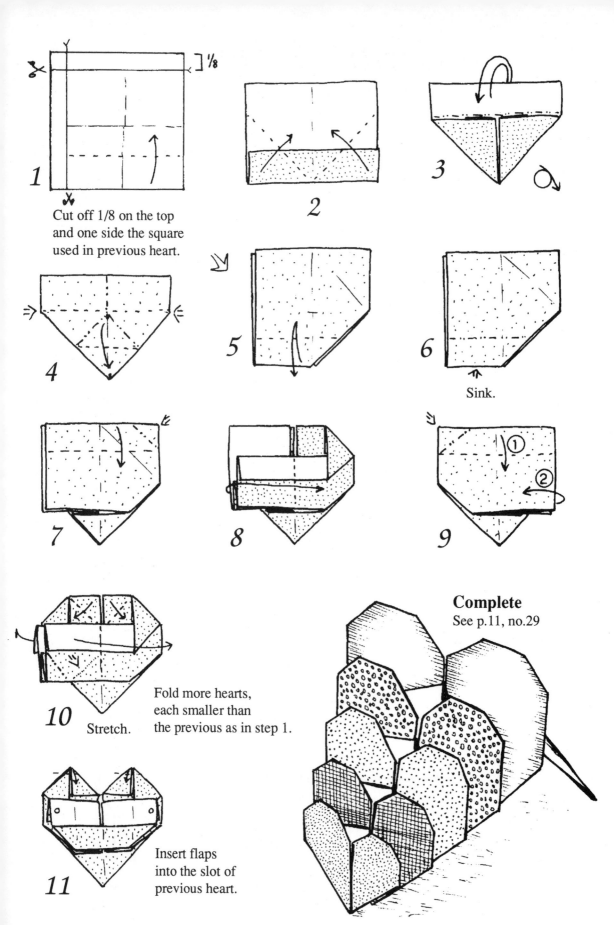

1

Cut off 1/8 on the top and one side the square used in previous heart.

2

3

4

5

6

Sink.

7

8

9

10

Stretch.

Fold more hearts, each smaller than the previous as in step 1.

11

Insert flaps into the slot of previous heart.

Complete
See p.11, no.29

30

Heart Frame

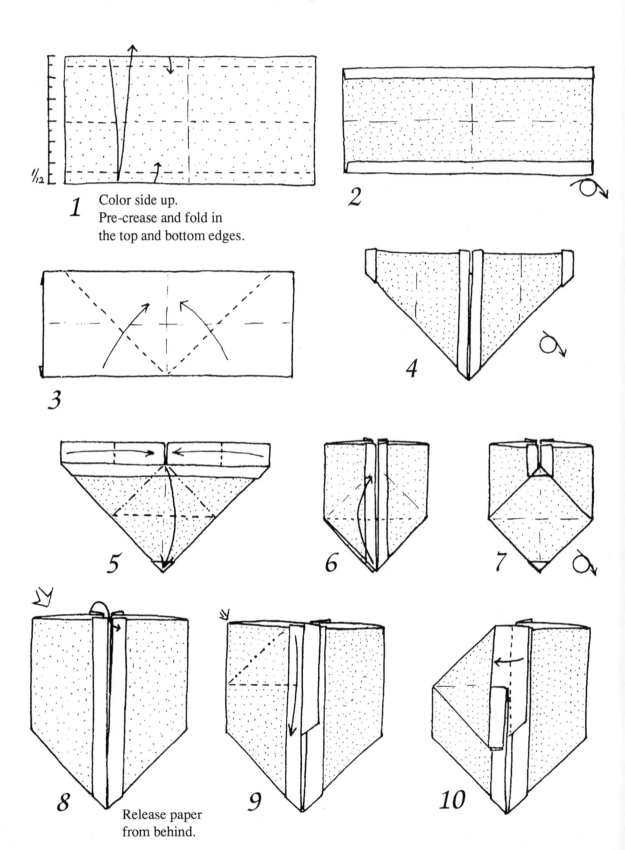

1 Color side up.
Pre-crease and fold in
the top and bottom edges.

2

3

4

5

6

7

8 Release paper
from behind.

9

10

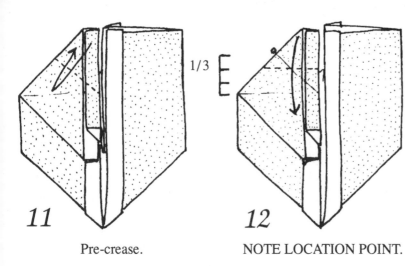

11 Pre-crease.

12 NOTE LOCATION POINT.

1/3

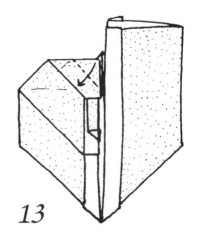

13

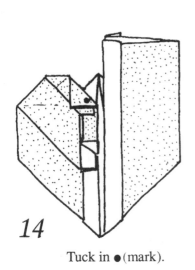

14 Tuck in ●(mark).

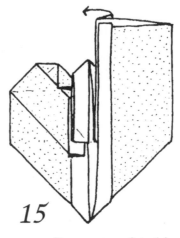

15 Repeat steps 8 to 14 for the right side.

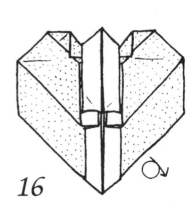

16

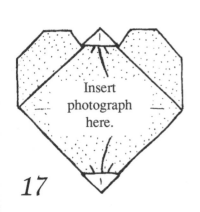

17 Insert photograph here.

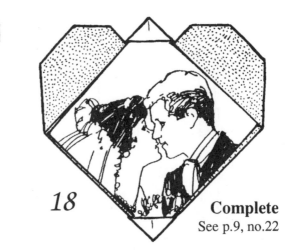

18 **Complete**
See p.9, no.22

Love Triangle

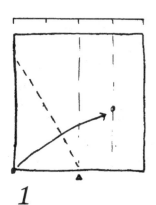

1

White side up.
Produce 60° creases.

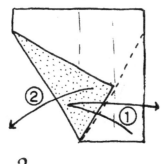

2

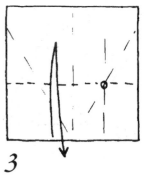

3

NOTE LOCATION POINTS.

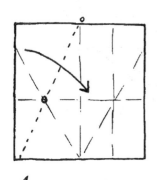

4

NOTE LOCATION POINTS.

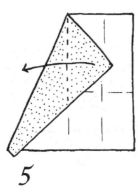

5

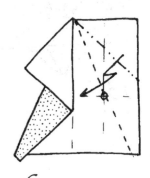

6

Repeat steps 4 and 5
for the right side.

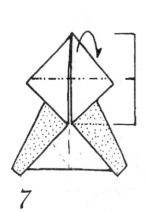

7

NOTE LOCATION POINTS.

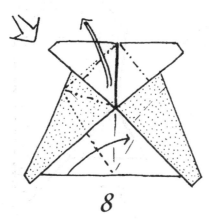

8

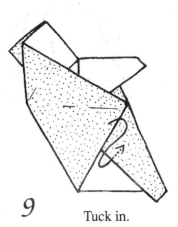

9

Tuck in.

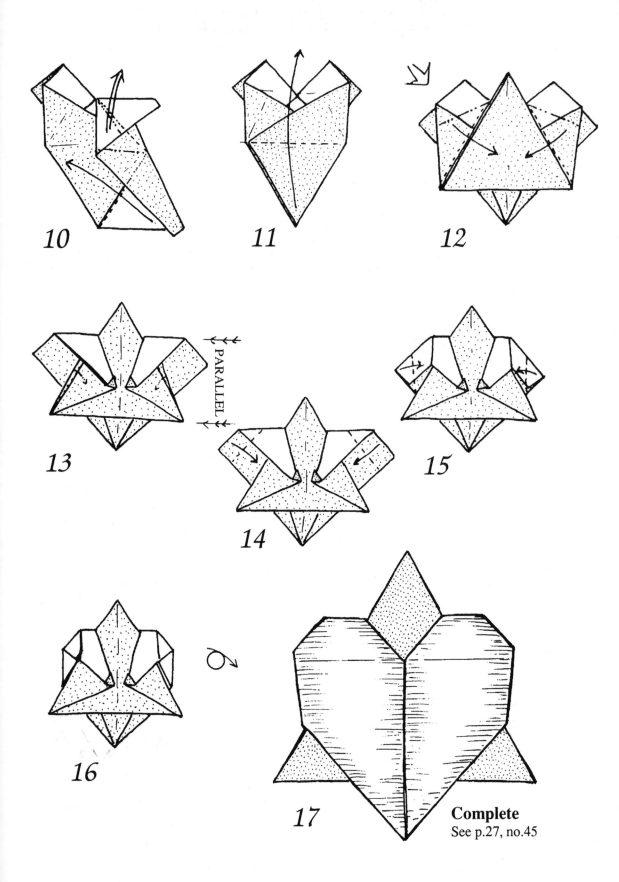

10

11

12

13

PARALLEL

14

15

16

17

Complete
See p.27, no.45

Flip-Over Heart

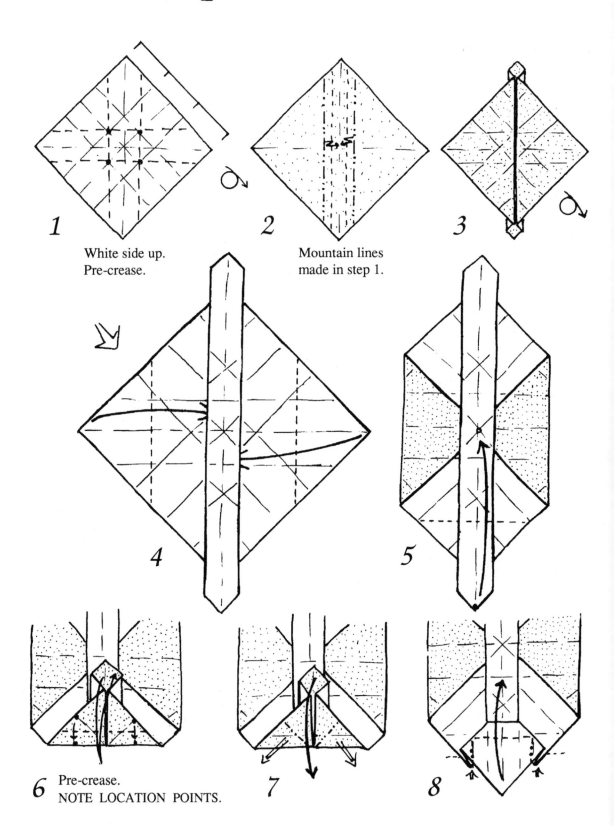

1
White side up.
Pre-crease.

2
Mountain lines
made in step 1.

3

4

5

6 Pre-crease.
NOTE LOCATION POINTS.

7

8

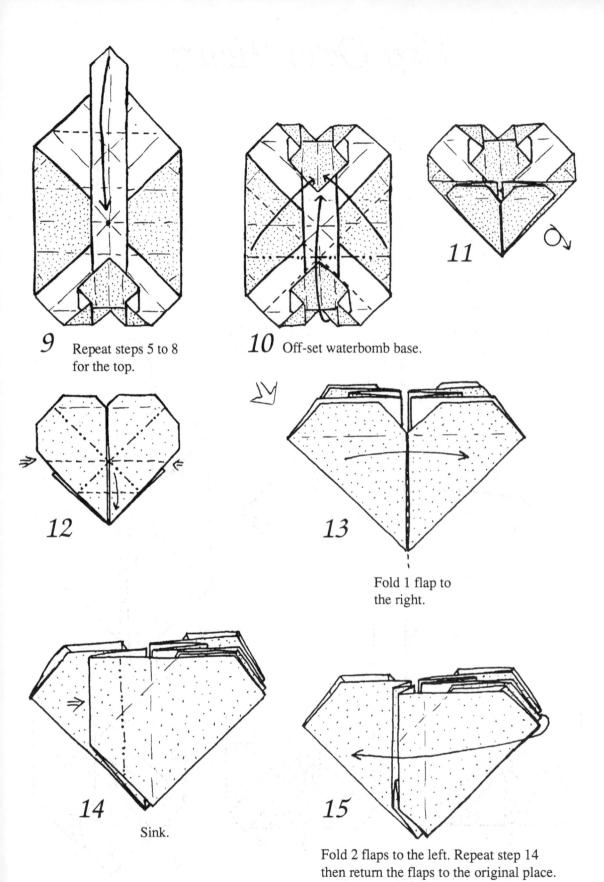

9 Repeat steps 5 to 8 for the top.

10 Off-set waterbomb base.

11

12

13 Fold 1 flap to the right.

14 Sink.

15 Fold 2 flaps to the left. Repeat step 14 then return the flaps to the original place.

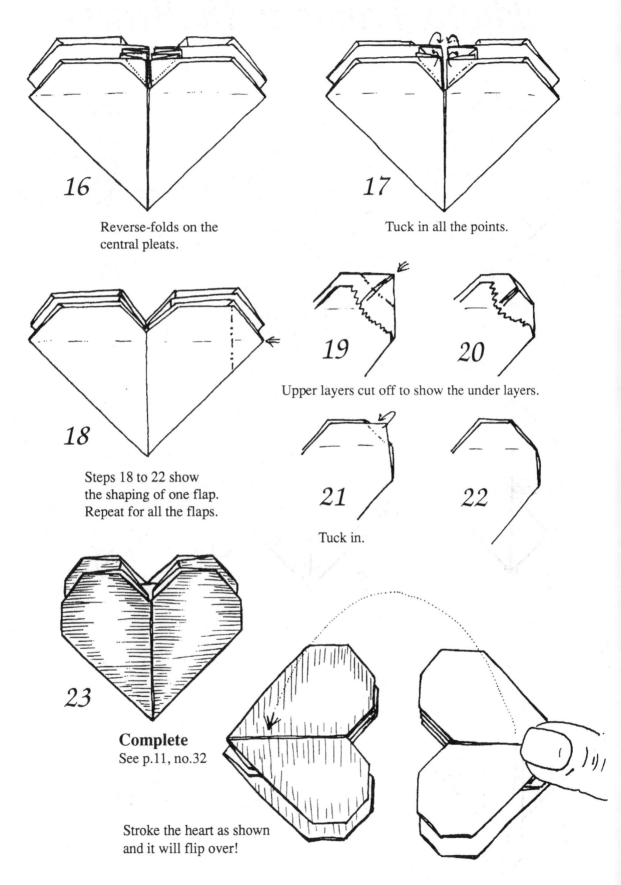

16

Reverse-folds on the
central pleats.

17

Tuck in all the points.

18

Steps 18 to 22 show
the shaping of one flap.
Repeat for all the flaps.

19

20

Upper layers cut off to show the under layers.

21

22

Tuck in.

23

Complete
See p.11, no.32

Stroke the heart as shown
and it will flip over!

Photo Frame with Hearts

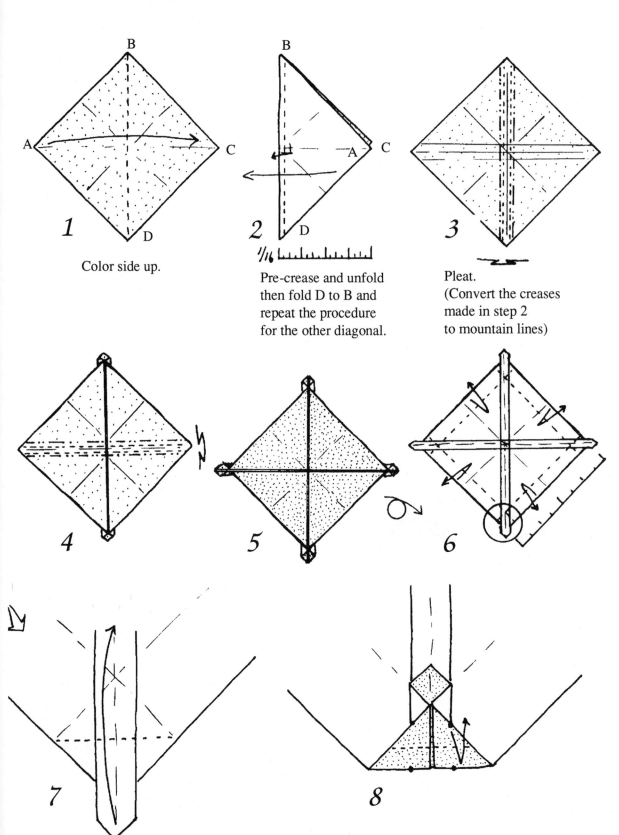

1
Color side up.

2
Pre-crease and unfold
then fold D to B and
repeat the procedure
for the other diagonal.

3
Pleat.
(Convert the creases
made in step 2
to mountain lines)

4

5

6

7

8

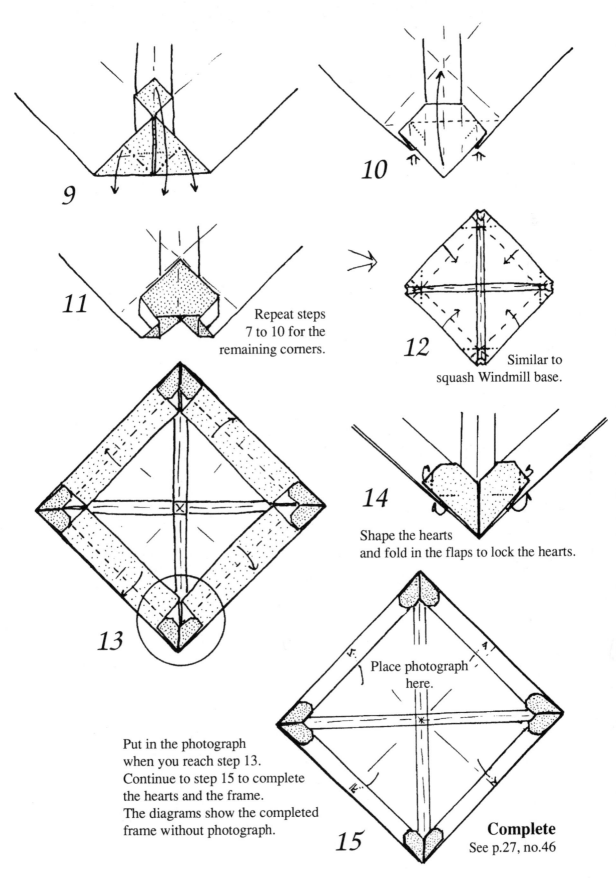

9

10

11 Repeat steps
7 to 10 for the
remaining corners.

12 Similar to
squash Windmill base.

13

14

Shape the hearts
and fold in the flaps to lock the hearts.

Put in the photograph
when you reach step 13.
Continue to step 15 to complete
the hearts and the frame.
The diagrams show the completed
frame without photograph.

Place photograph
here.

15

Complete
See p.27, no.46

A Gift of Love

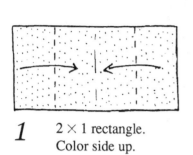

1   2 × 1 rectangle.
Color side up.

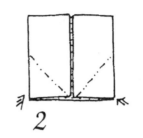

2

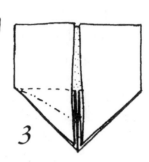

3

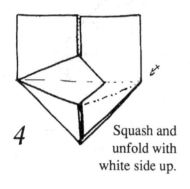

4   Squash and
unfold with
white side up.

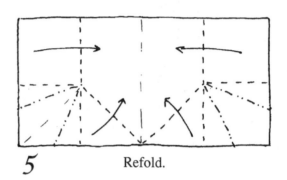

5   Refold.

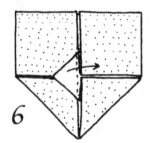

6

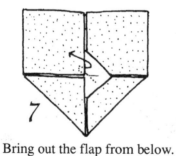

7

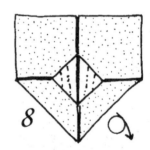

8

Bring out the flap from below.

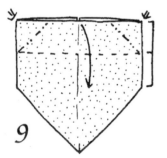

9

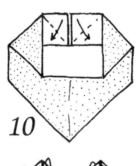

10

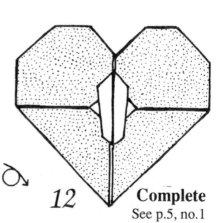

12   **Complete**
See p.5, no.1

11

40

Heart Ring 1

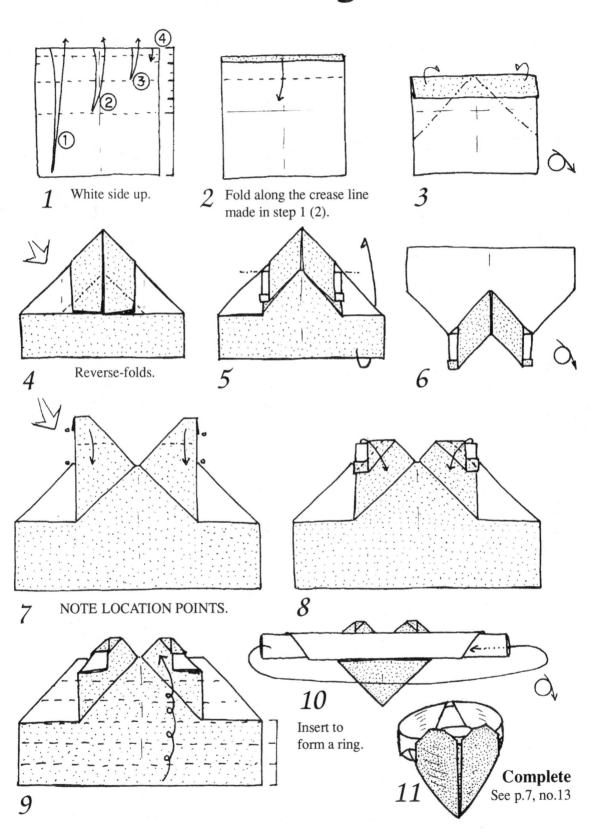

1 White side up.

2 Fold along the crease line made in step 1 (2).

3

4 Reverse-folds.

5

6

7 NOTE LOCATION POINTS.

8

9

10 Insert to form a ring.

11 **Complete** See p.7, no.13

Heart Ring 2

Model: David Petty
Drawings and
Modifications: Francis Ow

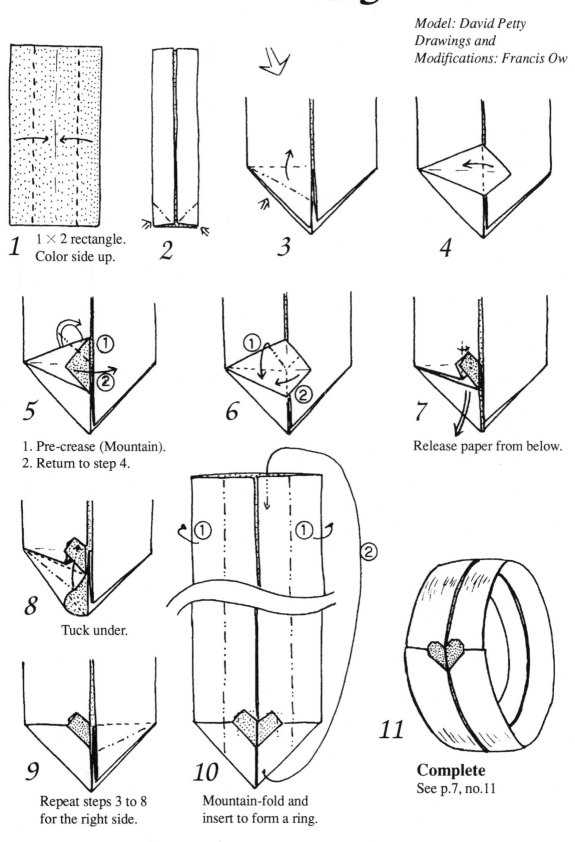

1 1 × 2 rectangle. Color side up.

2

3

4

5
1. Pre-crease (Mountain).
2. Return to step 4.

6

7 Release paper from below.

8 Tuck under.

9 Repeat steps 3 to 8 for the right side.

10 Mountain-fold and insert to form a ring.

11 **Complete**
See p.7, no.11

42

Bigamous

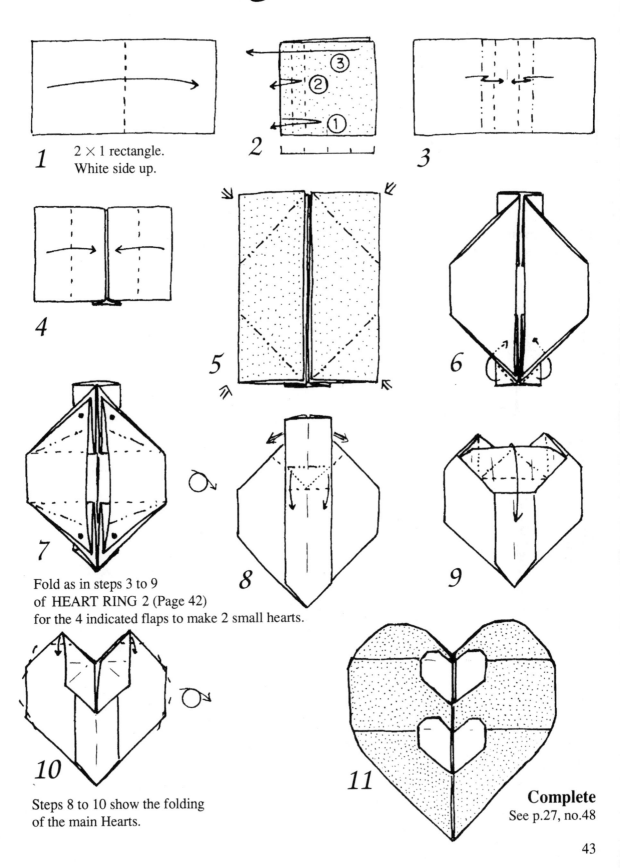

1 2 × 1 rectangle. White side up.

2

3

4

5

6

7 Fold as in steps 3 to 9 of HEART RING 2 (Page 42) for the 4 indicated flaps to make 2 small hearts.

8

9

10 Steps 8 to 10 show the folding of the main Hearts.

11 **Complete**
See p.27, no.48

Heart on Heart

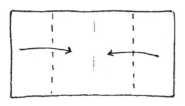

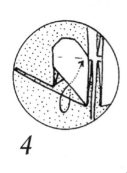

1 2 × 1 rectangle. White side up. Fold as in HEART RING 2 (Page 42).

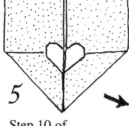

2 Step 7 of HEART RING 2 (Page 42). Shape the Heart as shown.

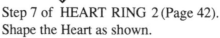

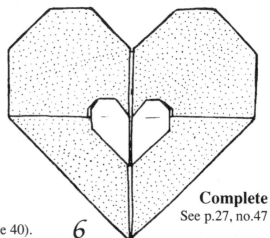

3

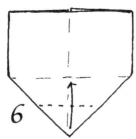

4

5 Step 10 of HEART RING 2. Turn over and fold the larger heart. Refer to steps 9 to 11 of A GIFT OF LOVE (Page 40).

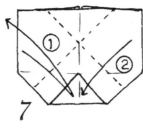

6

Complete
See p.27, no.47

Lover's Hat

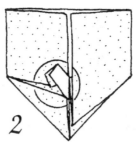

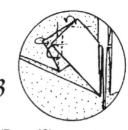

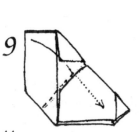

6

7

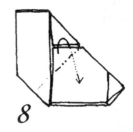

8

9

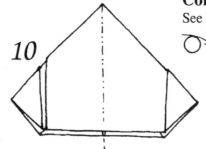

10

Complete
See p.6, no.6

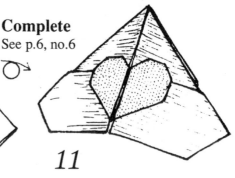

11

Love Cap

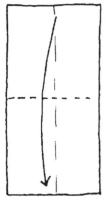

1 1 × 2 rectangle. White side up.

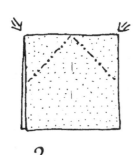

2

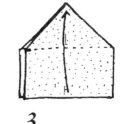

3

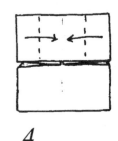

4

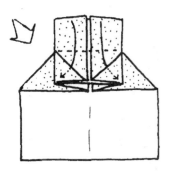

5 Fold down and tuck into pockets.

6

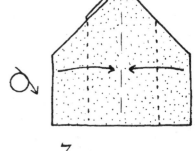

7

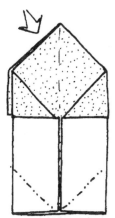

8 Form Heart. Refer to steps 3 to 9 of HEART RING 2 (Page 42).

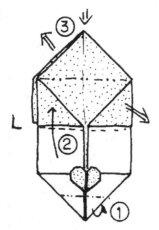

9
1. Mountain-fold.
2. Fold up 90˚.
3. Open to form the cap.

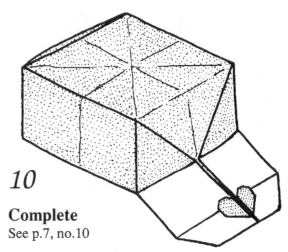

10

Complete
See p.7, no.10

45

Half-Hearted

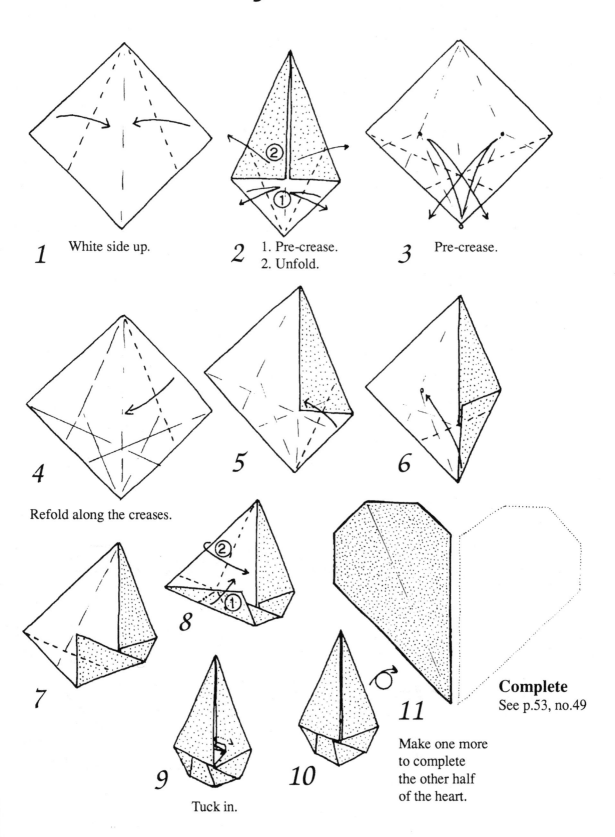

1 White side up.

2 1. Pre-crease.
2. Unfold.

3 Pre-crease.

4 Refold along the creases.

5

6

7

8

9 Tuck in.

10

11 Make one more
to complete
the other half
of the heart.

Complete
See p.53, no.49

Pockets for Half-Hearted

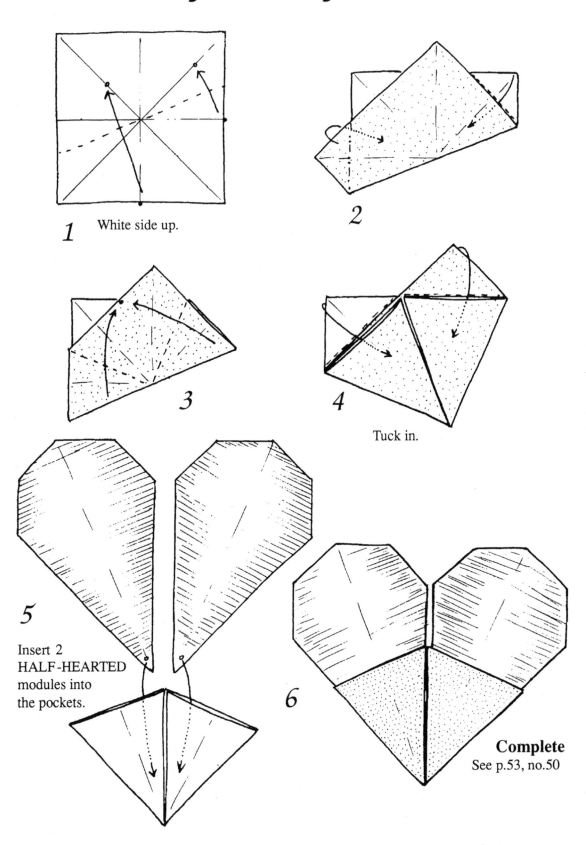

1 White side up.

2

3

4 Tuck in.

5

Insert 2
HALF-HEARTED
modules into
the pockets.

6

Complete
See p.53, no.50

A Better Half

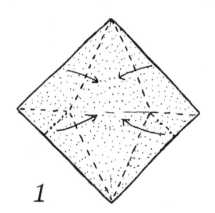

1

Color side up
or use "Duo-colored" Paper.

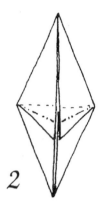

2

FISH BASE.
Squash the 2 flaps
and fold the heart
as in steps 3 to 10
of HEART RING 2
(Page 42).

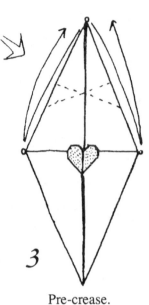

3

Pre-crease.

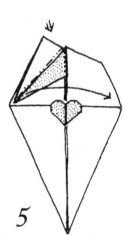

4

Reverse.

5

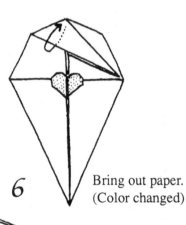

6

Bring out paper.
(Color changed)

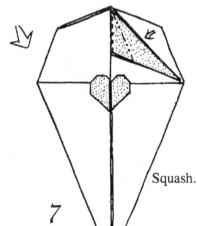

7

Squash.

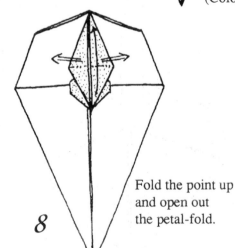

8

Fold the point up
and open out
the petal-fold.

Coaster

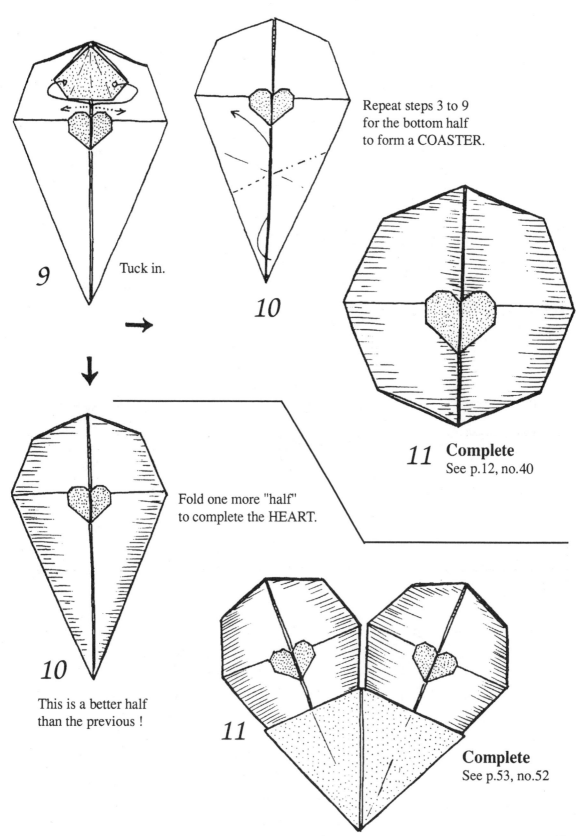

9 Tuck in.

Repeat steps 3 to 9 for the bottom half to form a COASTER.

10

11 Complete
See p.12, no.40

10 This is a better half than the previous !

Fold one more "half" to complete the HEART.

11

Complete
See p.53, no.52

Dutch Valentine Card

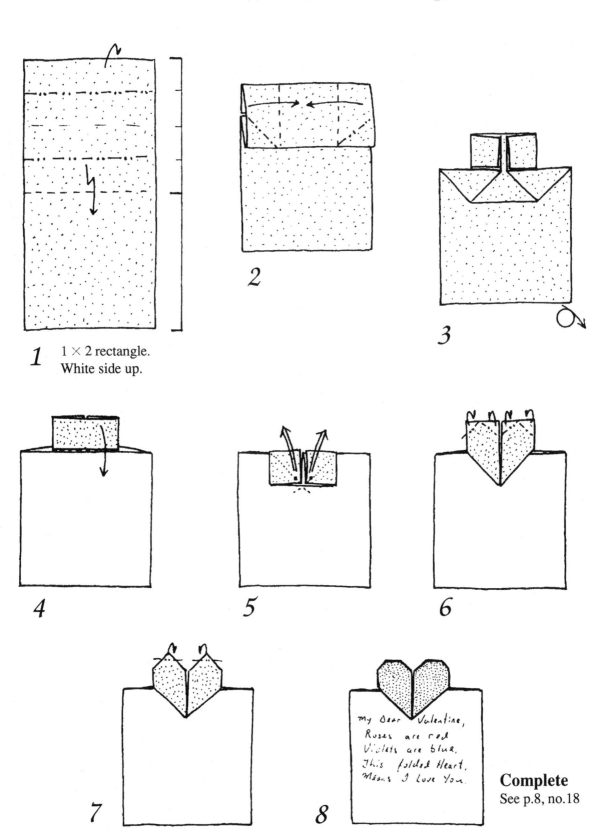

1 1 × 2 rectangle.
White side up.

2

3

4

5

6

7

8 My Dear Valentine,
Roses are red
Violets are blue.
This folded Heart,
Means I love You.

Complete
See p.8, no.18

50

Box

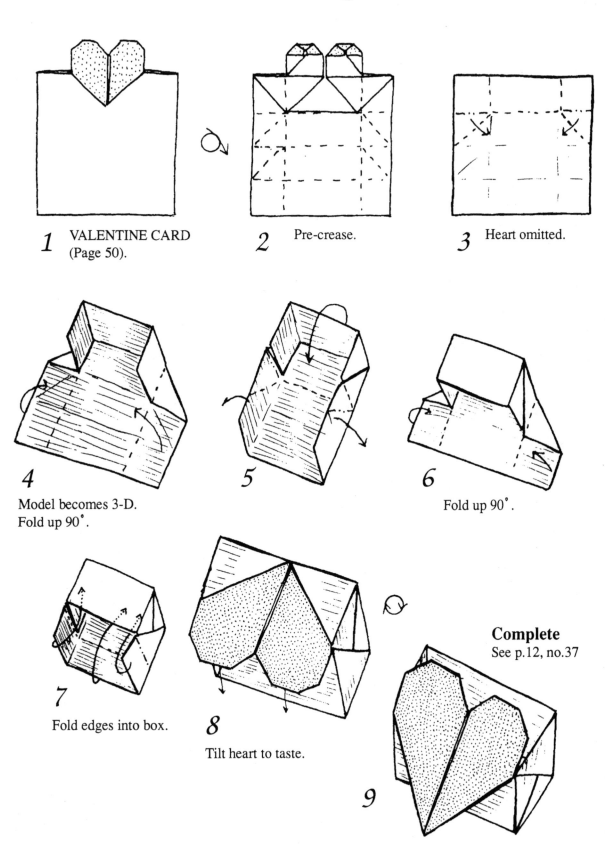

1 VALENTINE CARD (Page 50).

2 Pre-crease.

3 Heart omitted.

4 Model becomes 3-D. Fold up 90°.

5

6 Fold up 90°.

7 Fold edges into box.

8 Tilt heart to taste.

9

Complete
See p.12, no.37

51

Love on the Rock

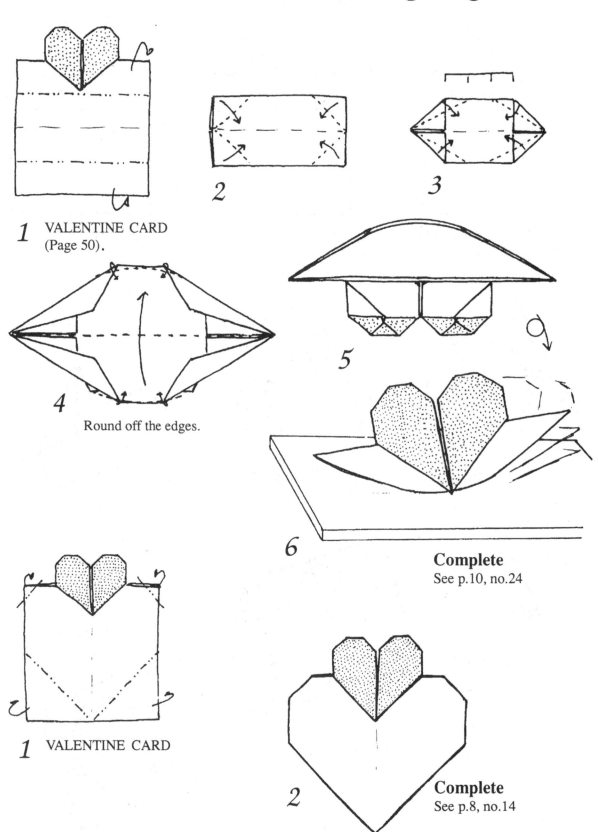

1 VALENTINE CARD
(Page 50).

2

3

4 Round off the edges.

5

6

Complete
See p.10, no.24

1 VALENTINE CARD

2

Complete
See p.8, no.14

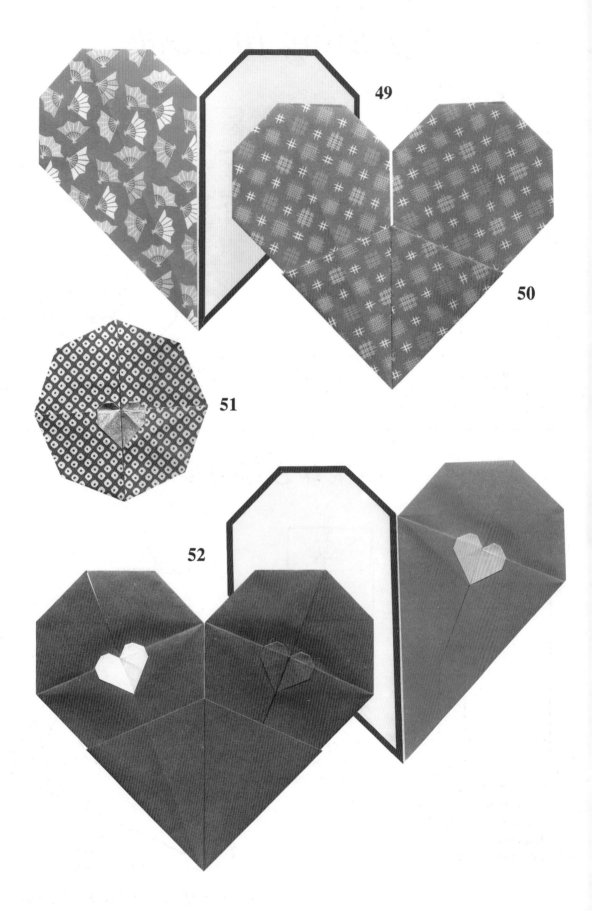

49

50

51

52

Falling in Love

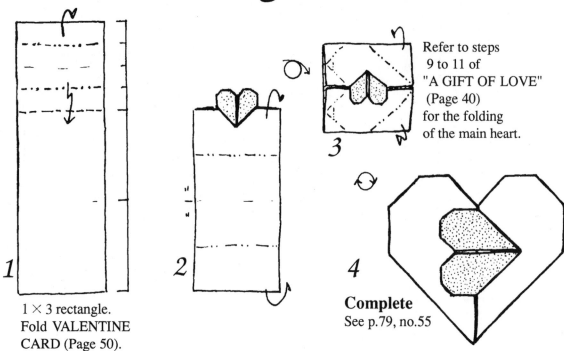

1

1×3 rectangle.
Fold VALENTINE
CARD (Page 50).

2

3

Refer to steps
9 to 11 of
"A GIFT OF LOVE"
(Page 40)
for the folding
of the main heart.

4

Complete
See p.79, no.55

On a Stand

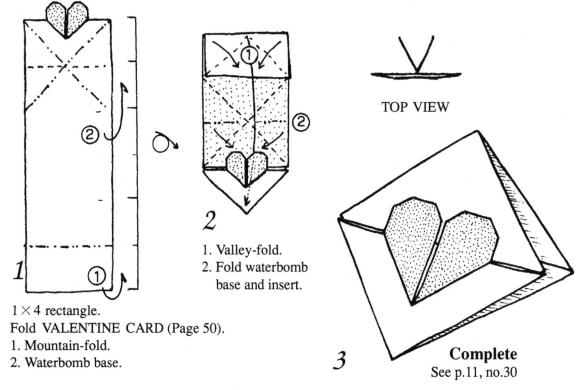

1

1×4 rectangle.
Fold VALENTINE CARD (Page 50).
1. Mountain-fold.
2. Waterbomb base.

2

1. Valley-fold.
2. Fold waterbomb
   base and insert.

TOP VIEW

3

Complete
See p.11, no.30

Fold up the flaps from behind to form the stand.

2's Company, 3's a Crowd

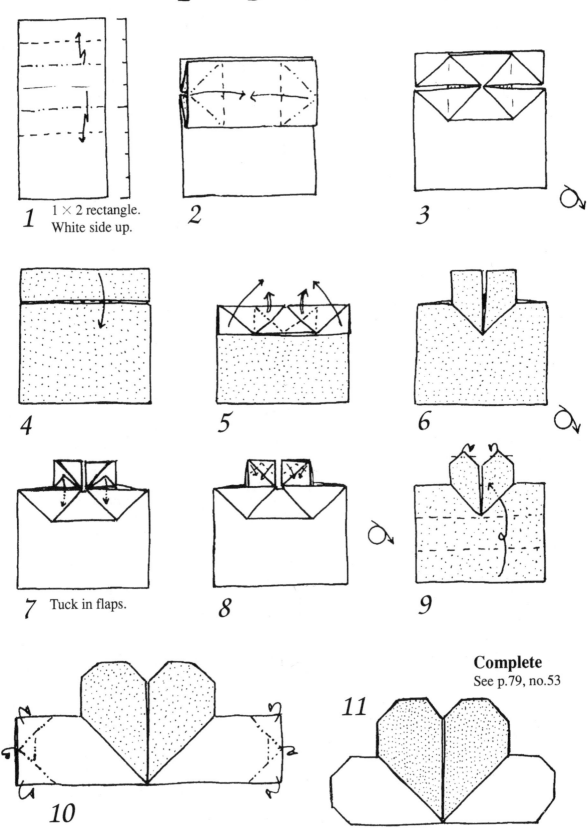

1 1 × 2 rectangle. White side up.

2

3

4

5

6

7 Tuck in flaps.

8

9

10

11

Complete
See p.79, no.53

4's Too Many, 8's an Orgy

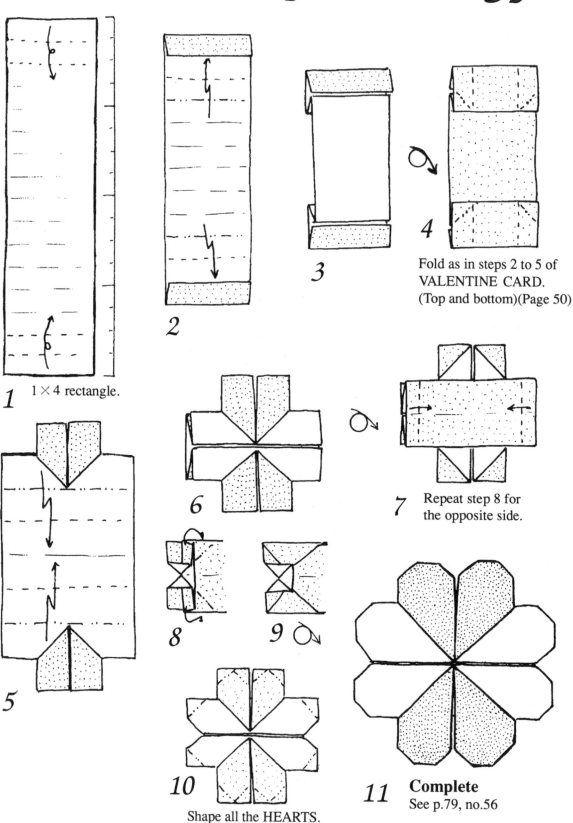

1 1 × 4 rectangle.

2

3

4 Fold as in steps 2 to 5 of VALENTINE CARD. (Top and bottom)(Page 50)

5

6

7 Repeat step 8 for the opposite side.

8

9

10 Shape all the HEARTS.

11 **Complete**
See p.79, no.56

Heart Envelope

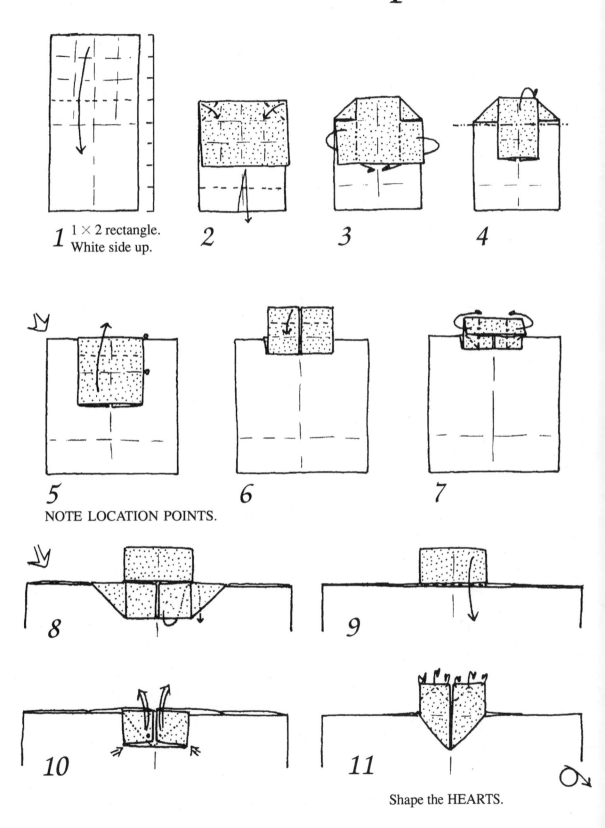

1 1 × 2 rectangle. White side up.

2

3

4

5 NOTE LOCATION POINTS.

6

7

8

9

10

11 Shape the HEARTS.

57

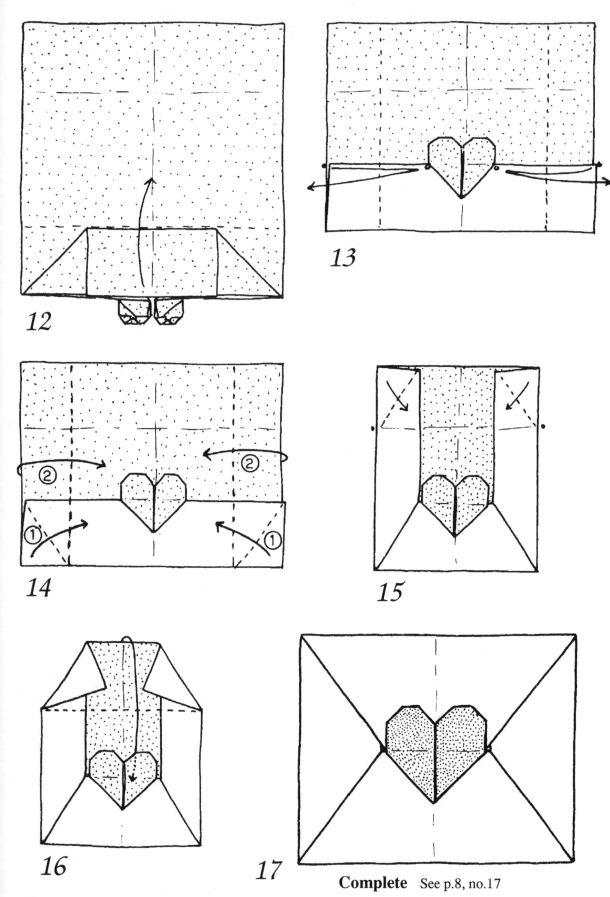

12

13

14

15

16

17

Complete   See p.8, no.17

Sweet Heart

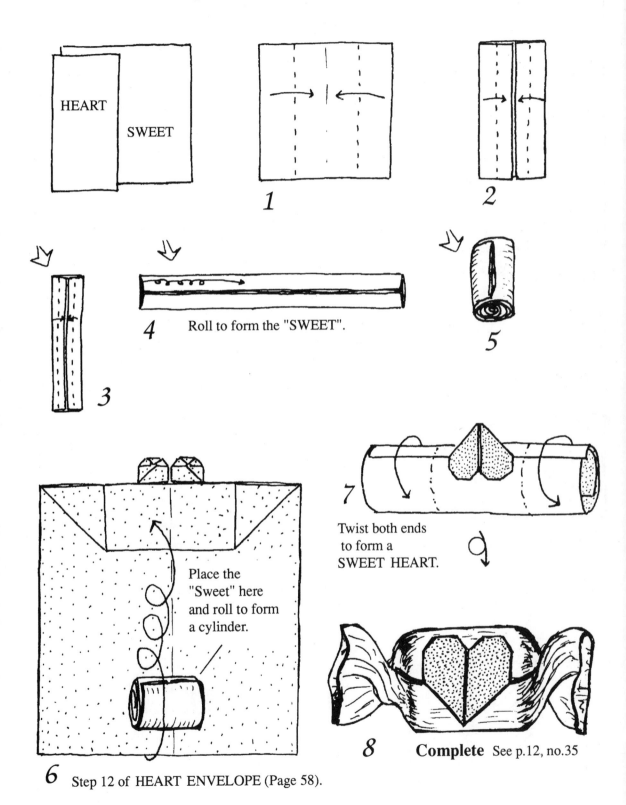

HEART

SWEET

1

2

3

4 Roll to form the "SWEET".

5

6 Step 12 of HEART ENVELOPE (Page 58).

Place the "Sweet" here and roll to form a cylinder.

7 Twist both ends to form a SWEET HEART.

8 **Complete** See p.12, no.35

Try using real candy for this model !

Love Boxes

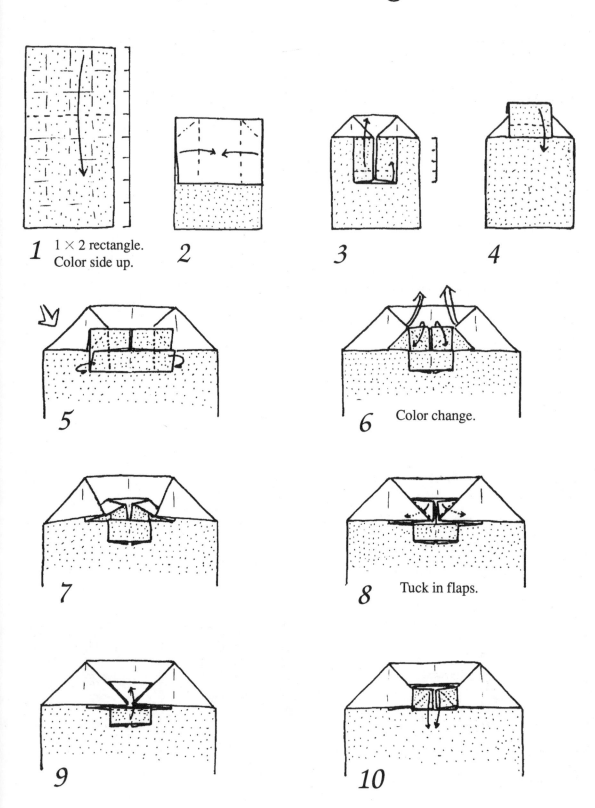

1 1 × 2 rectangle.
Color side up.

2

3

4

5

6 Color change.

7

8 Tuck in flaps.

9

10

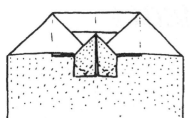

11 Shape the Heart.

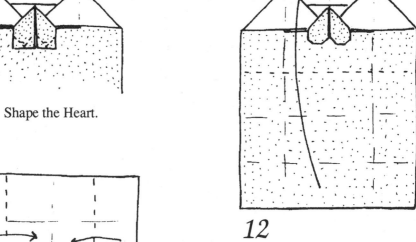

12

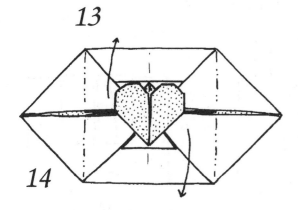

Repeat steps 2 to 11 for the bottom half.

13

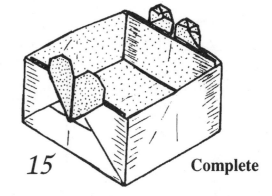

14

15 **Complete**

VARIATION

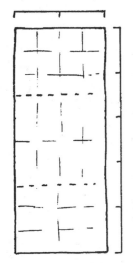

2 × 5 rectangle.

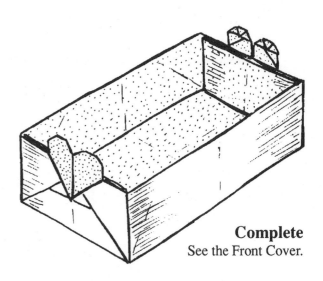

Complete
See the Front Cover.

Flowery Heart

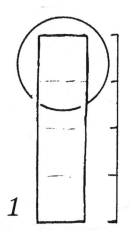

1

1 × 4 rectangle.
White side up.

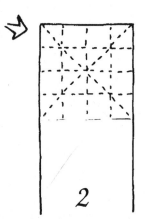

2

Pre-crease.

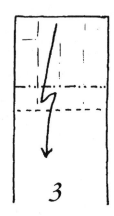

3

Pleat.

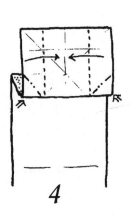

4

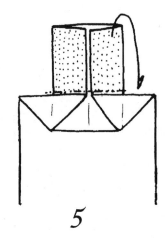

5

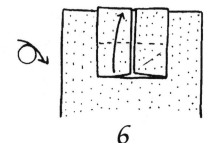

6

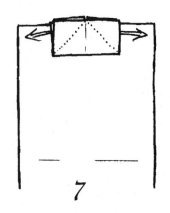

7

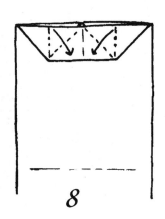

8

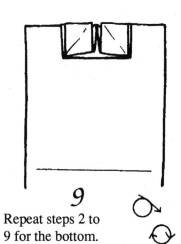

9

Repeat steps 2 to
9 for the bottom.

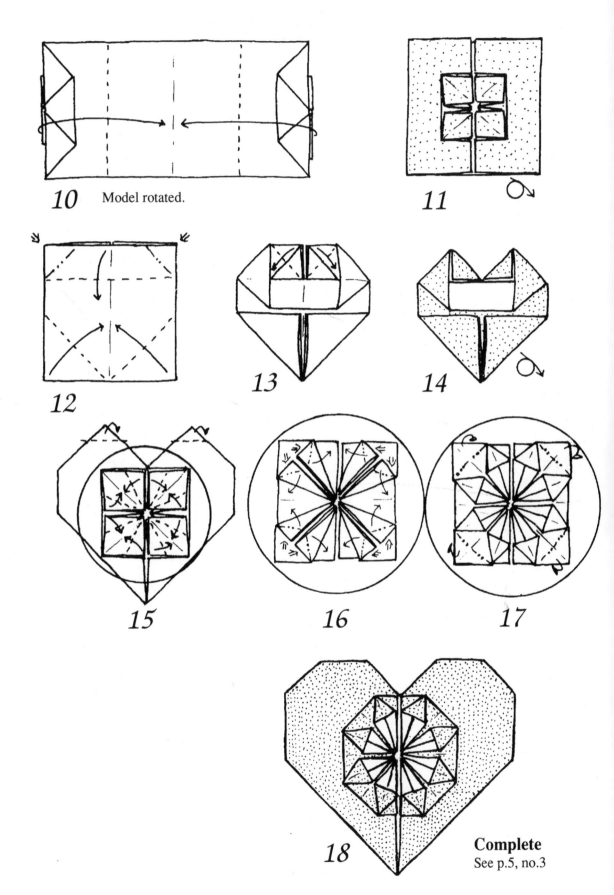

10 Model rotated.

11

12

13

14

15

16

17

18 **Complete**
See p.5, no.3

Heart ["Fuse" Lock]

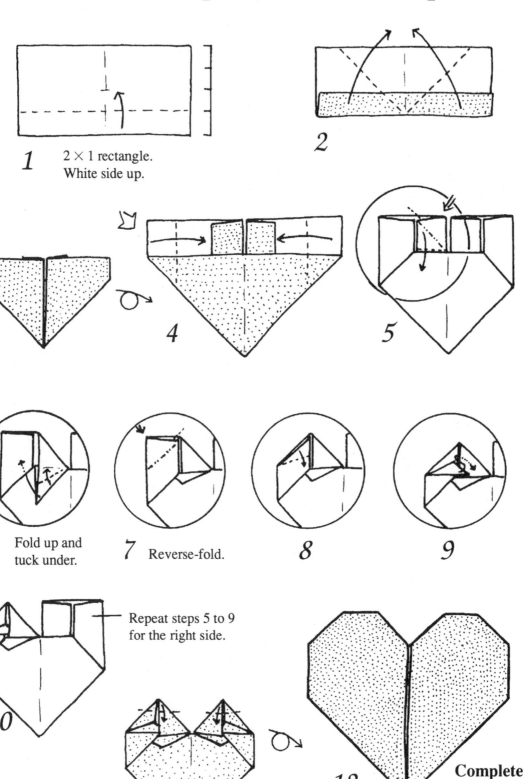

1 2 × 1 rectangle.
White side up.

2

3

4

5

6 Fold up and
tuck under.

7 Reverse-fold.

8

9

10

Repeat steps 5 to 9
for the right side.

11

12 **Complete**
See p.79, no.59

64

Spring Heart

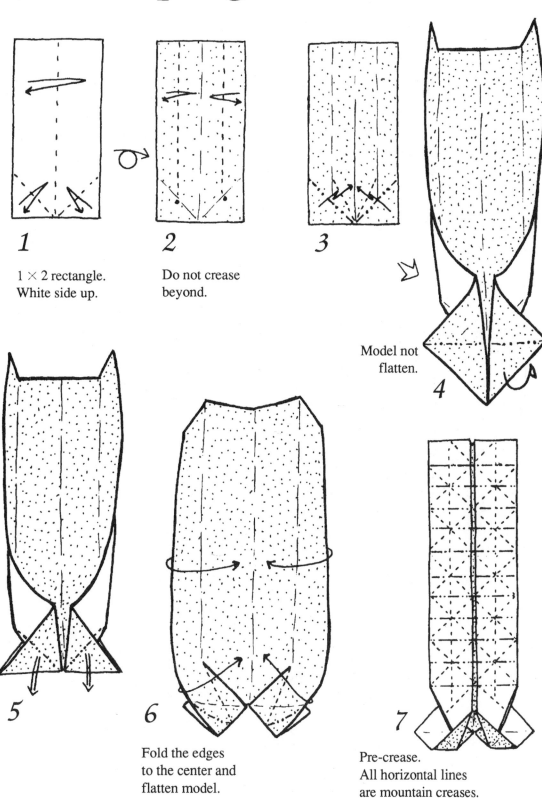

1

1 × 2 rectangle.
White side up.

2

Do not crease
beyond.

3

4

Model not
flatten.

5

6

Fold the edges
to the center and
flatten model.

7

Pre-crease.
All horizontal lines
are mountain creases.

Box-pleat to form the "Spring".

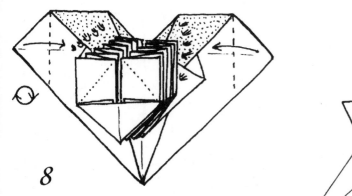

8

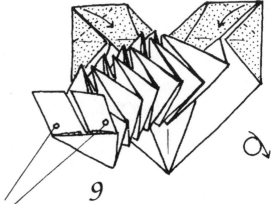

9

Insert into the slot
of the previous heart.

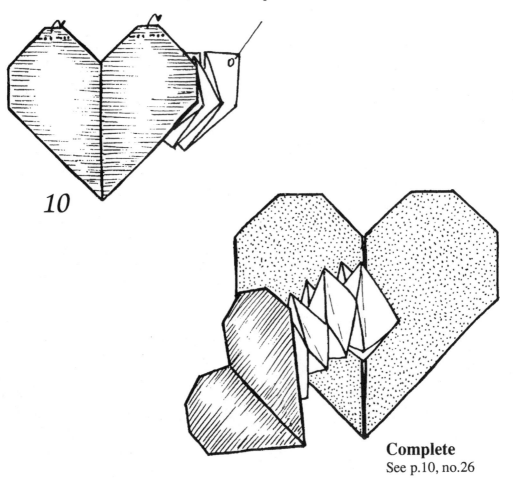

10

Complete
See p.10, no.26

Windmill on Heart

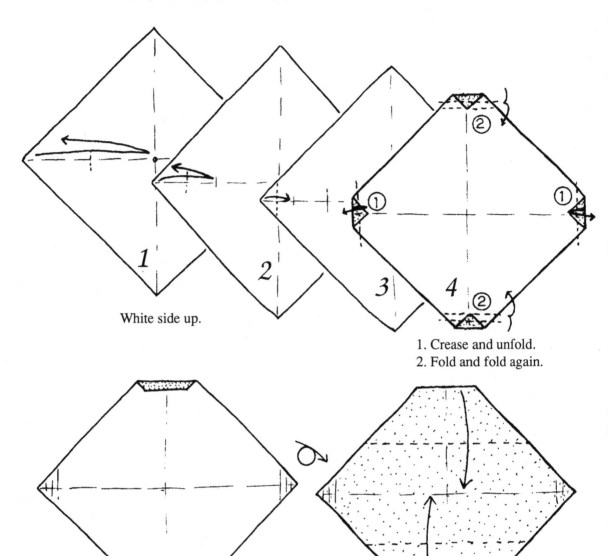

1

White side up.

2

3

4

1. Crease and unfold.
2. Fold and fold again.

5

6

7

8

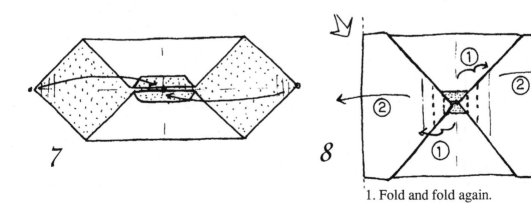

1. Fold and fold again.
2. Unfold.

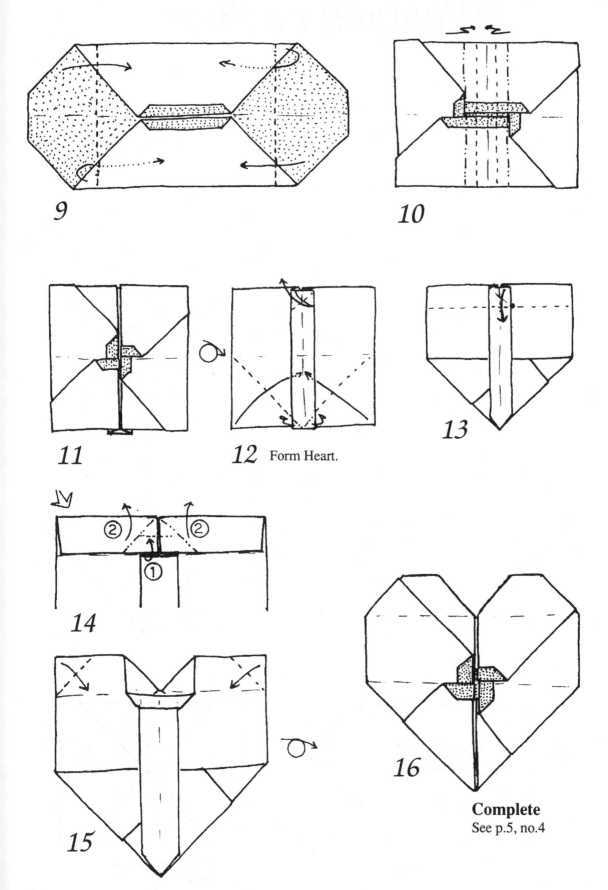

9

10

11

12 Form Heart.

13

14

15

16

Complete
See p.5, no.4

Baby Love

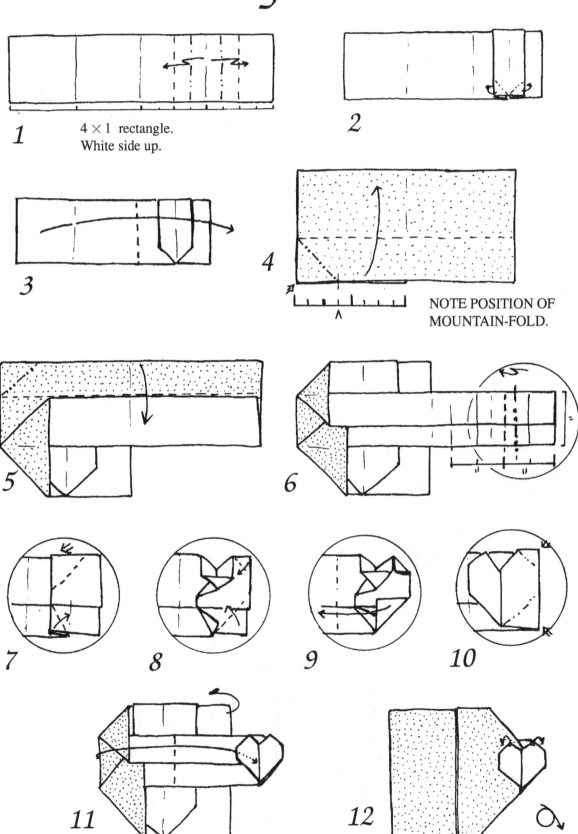

1 4×1 rectangle. White side up.

2

3

4 NOTE POSITION OF MOUNTAIN-FOLD.

5

6

7

8

9

10

11

12

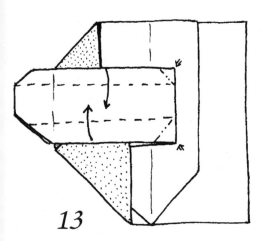

13

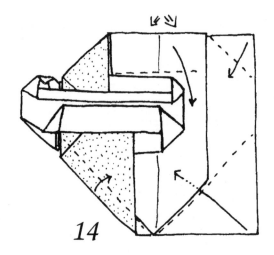

14

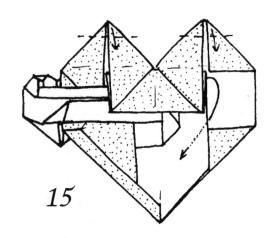

15

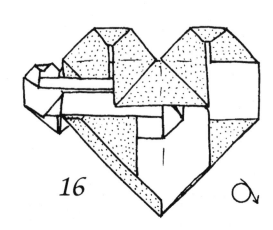

16

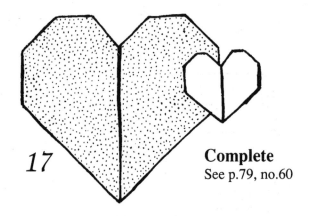

17

Complete
See p.79, no.60

Puppy Love

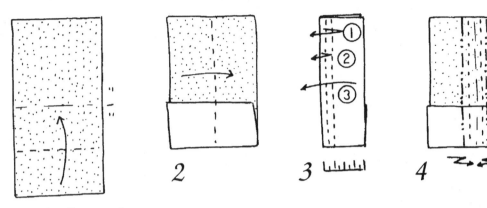

1 1 × 2 rectangle.
Color side up.

2

3

4

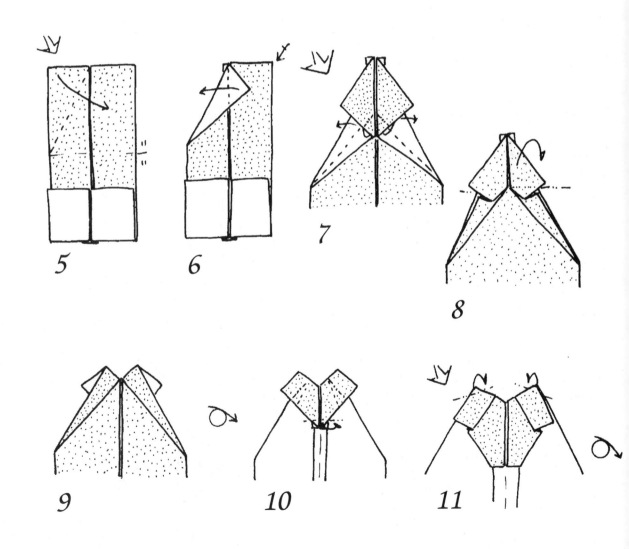

5

6

7

8

9

10

11

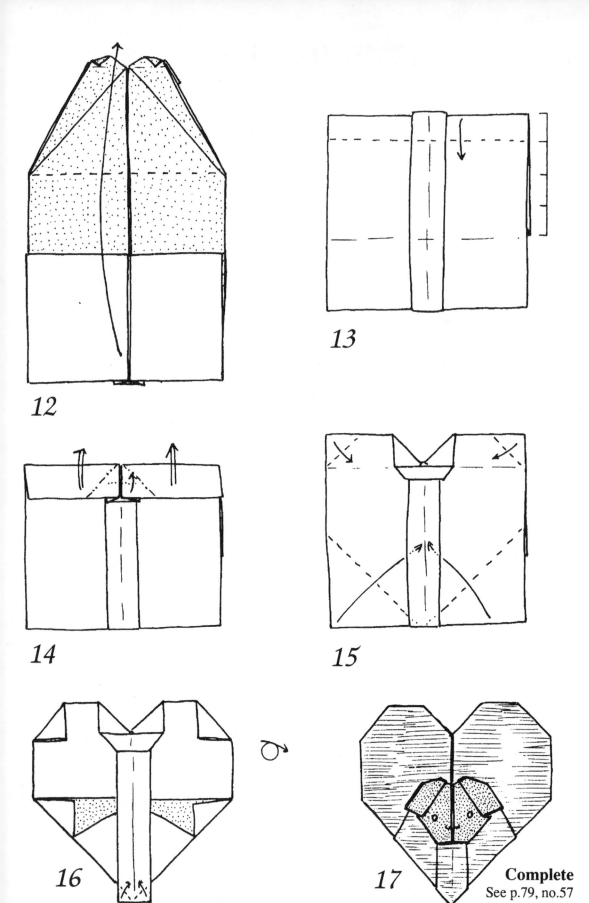

12

13

14

15

16

17 **Complete**
See p.79, no.57

Loving Pajaritas

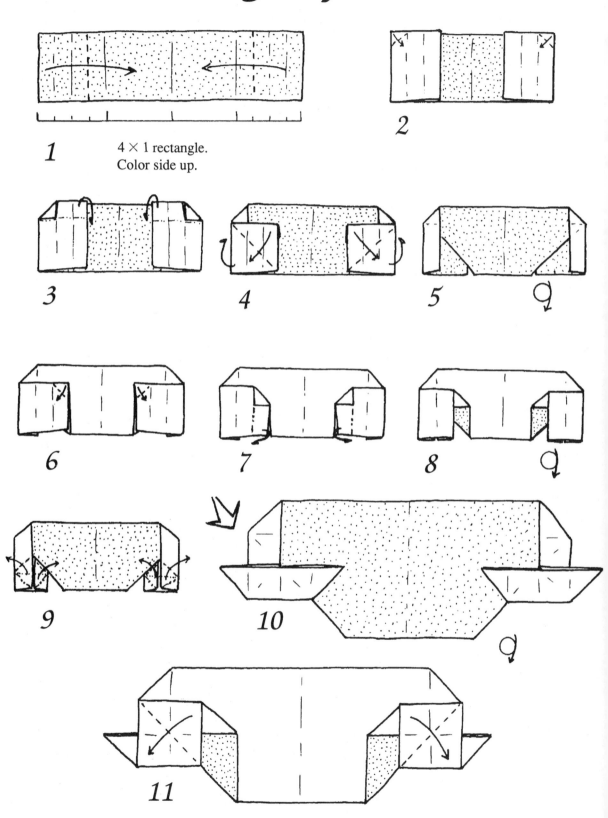

1 4 × 1 rectangle. Color side up.

2

3

4

5 ♀

6

7

8 ♀

9

10 ♀

11

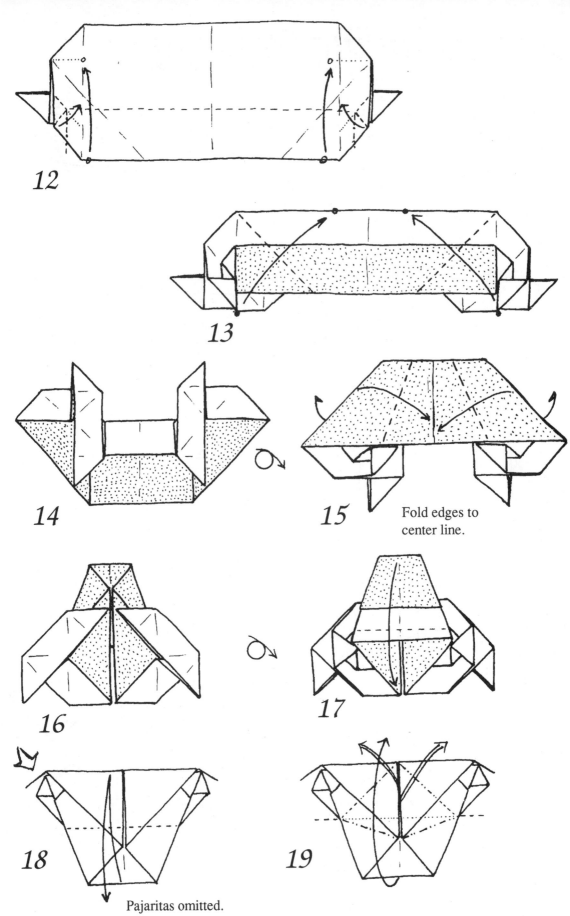

12

13

14

15 Fold edges to center line.

16

17

18 Pajaritas omitted.

19

74

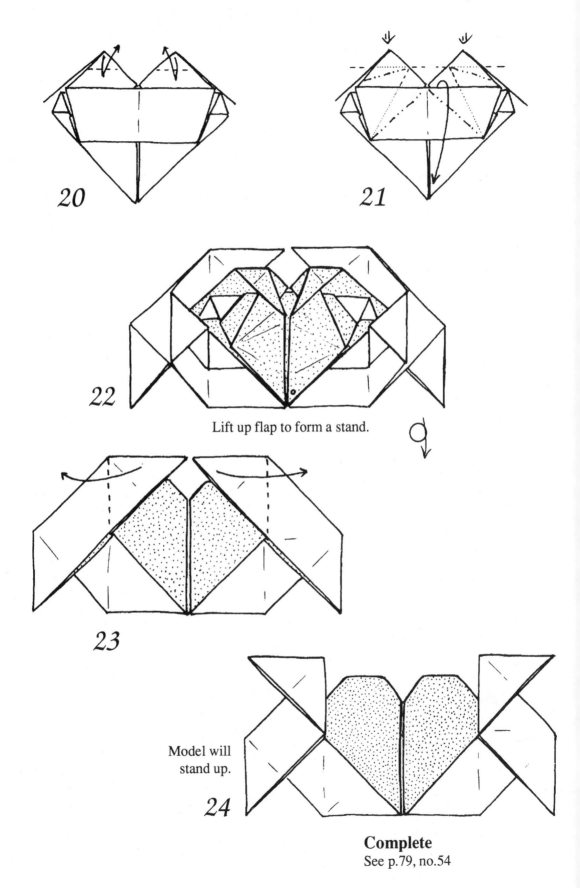

20

21

22

Lift up flap to form a stand.

23

Model will
stand up.

24

Complete
See p.79, no.54

Heart Tatou

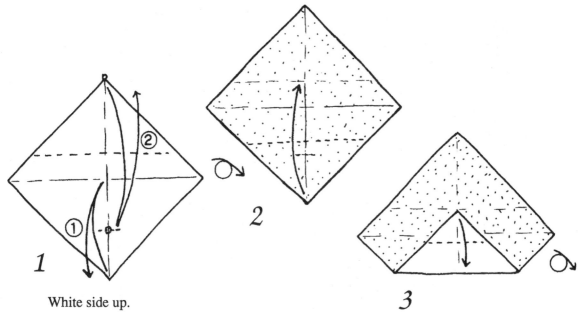

2

3

White side up.
1. Crease to mark.
2. Fold to crease
   mark made in 1.

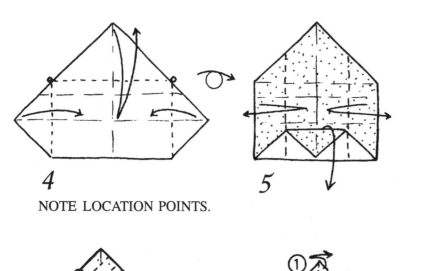

4

NOTE LOCATION POINTS.

5

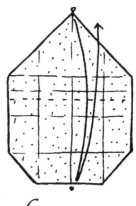

6

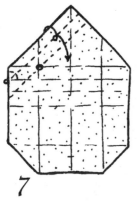

7

NOTE LOCATION POINTS.

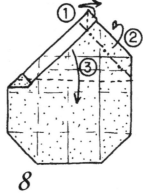

8

9

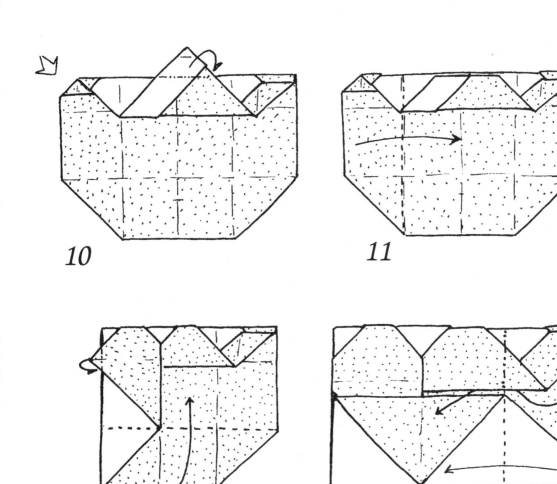

10

11

12

13

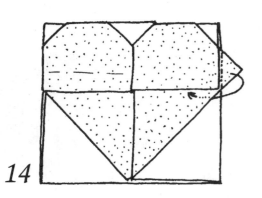

14

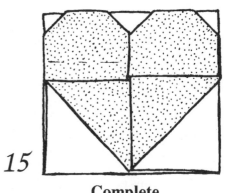

15

Complete
See p.12, no.39

Model by Jun Maekawa

Heart Pin

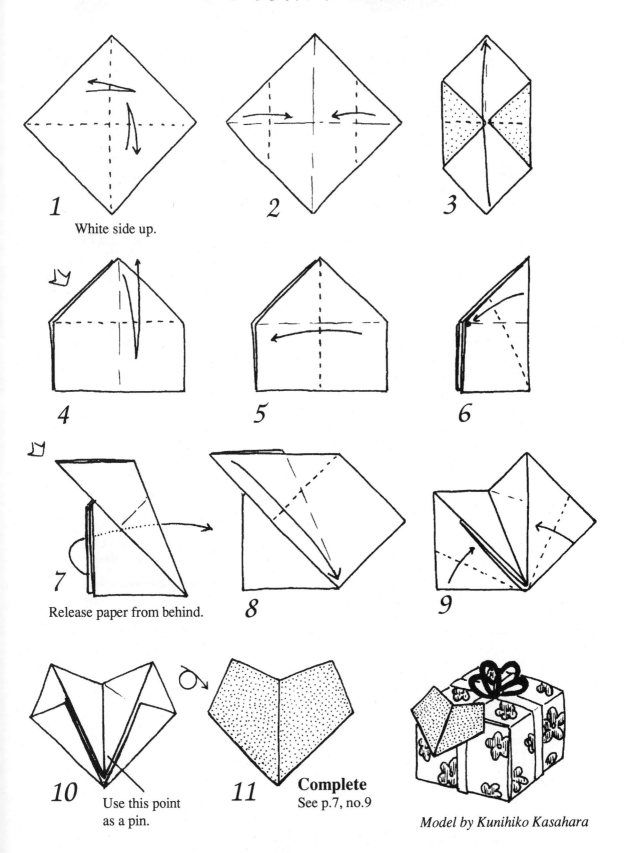

1 White side up.

2

3

4

5

6

7 Release paper from behind.

8

9

10 Use this point as a pin.

11 **Complete** See p.7, no.9

Model by Kunihiko Kasahara

78

53

54

55

56

57

58

59

60

61

Double-Sided Heart

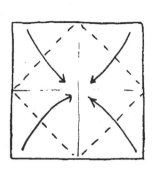

1 White side up.

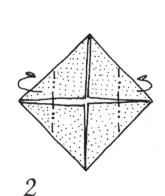

2

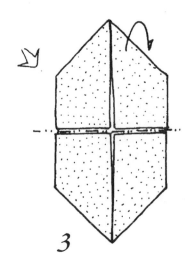

3

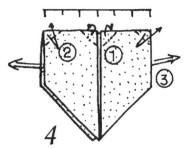

4

1. Mountain-fold.
2. Crease.
3. Unfold.

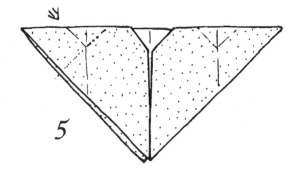

5

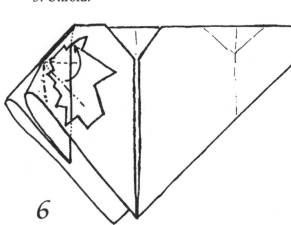

6

Model cut off to show the folds inside.
Repeat for the right side.

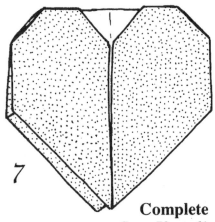

7

Complete
See p.79, no.61

Model: Nick Robinson
Drawings: Francis Ow

Heart on Pyramid

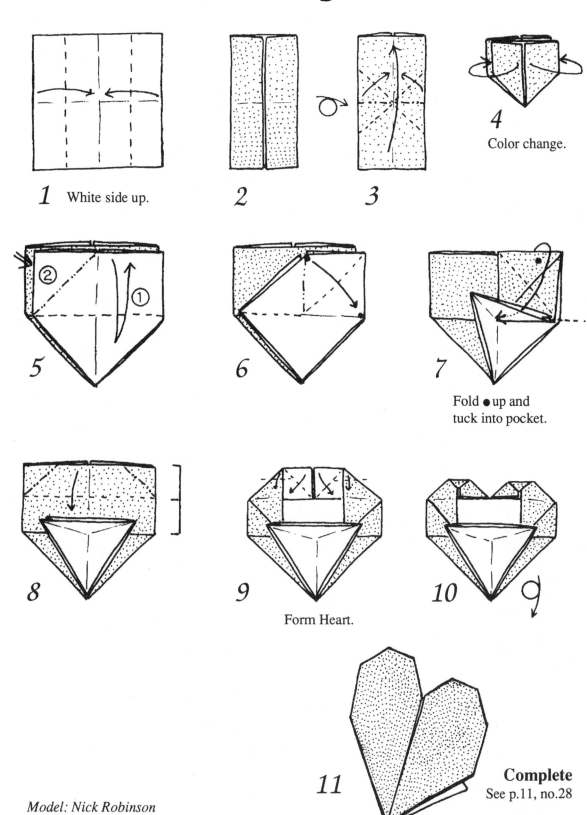

1 White side up.

2

3

4 Color change.

5

6

7 Fold ● up and tuck into pocket.

8

9 Form Heart.

10

11 **Complete**
See p.11, no.28

Model: Nick Robinson
Drawings: Francis Ow

Heart Module 6

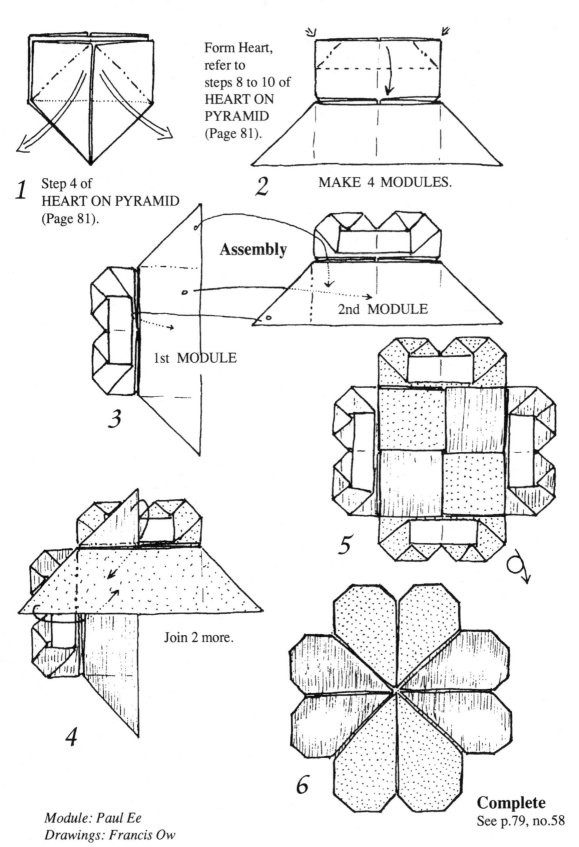

Form Heart, refer to steps 8 to 10 of **HEART ON PYRAMID** (Page 81).

1 Step 4 of HEART ON PYRAMID (Page 81).

2 MAKE 4 MODULES.

Assembly

1st MODULE

2nd MODULE

3

4 Join 2 more.

5

6

Complete
See p.79, no.58

Module: Paul Ee
Drawings: Francis Ow

3-D Heart (Petty's)

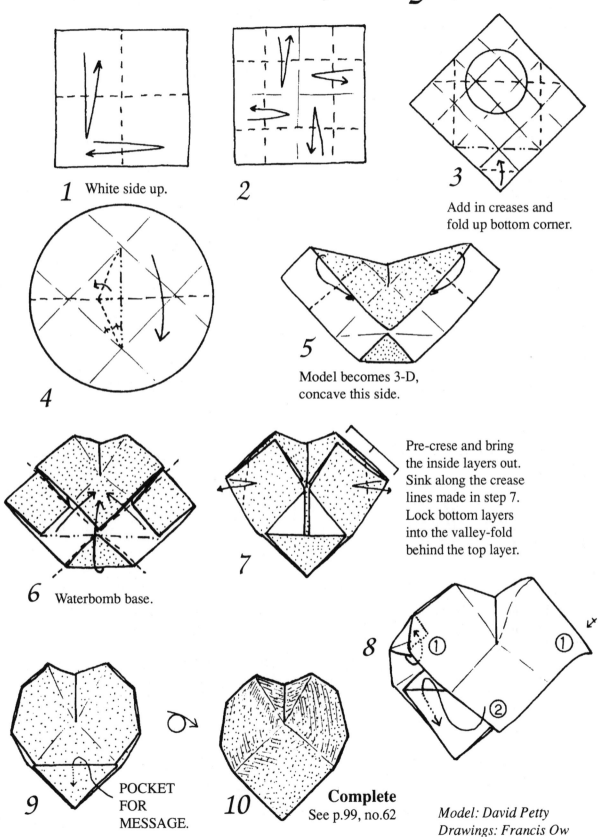

1 White side up.

2

3 Add in creases and fold up bottom corner.

4

5 Model becomes 3-D, concave this side.

6 Waterbomb base.

7 Pre-crese and bring the inside layers out. Sink along the crease lines made in step 7. Lock bottom layers into the valley-fold behind the top layer.

8 ① ① ②

9 POCKET FOR MESSAGE.

10 **Complete** See p.99, no.62

Model: David Petty
Drawings: Francis Ow

Head Over Heels

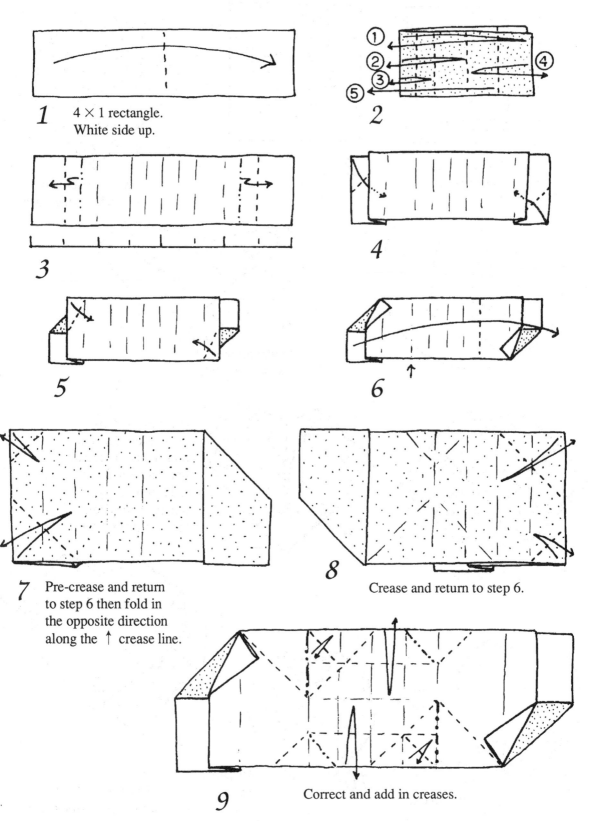

1 4 × 1 rectangle.
White side up.

2

3

4

5

6

7 Pre-crease and return
to step 6 then fold in
the opposite direction
along the ↑ crease line.

8 Crease and return to step 6.

9 Correct and add in creases.

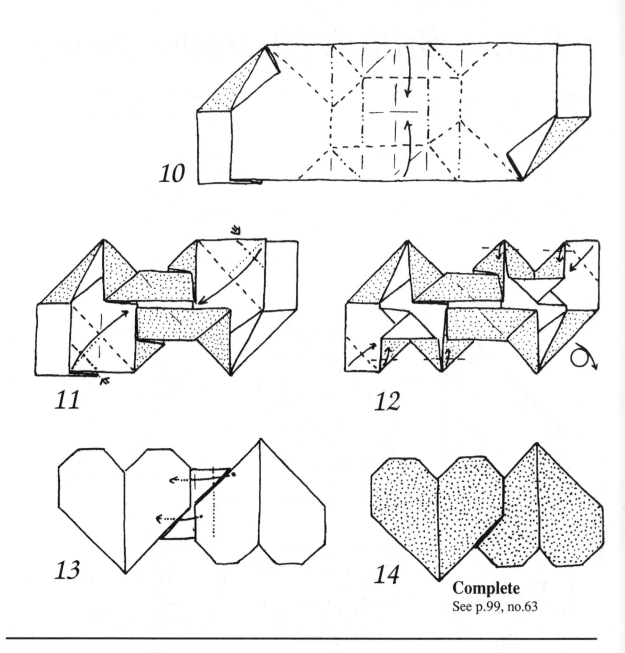

10

11

12

13

14 **Complete**
See p.99, no.63

Variation

1 6 × 1 rectangle.

2

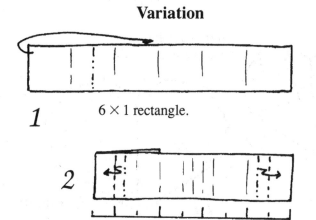

Complete

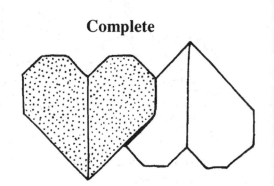

Heart Brooch [Accroche Coeur]

Model: Francois Ziegler
Drawings: Francis Ow

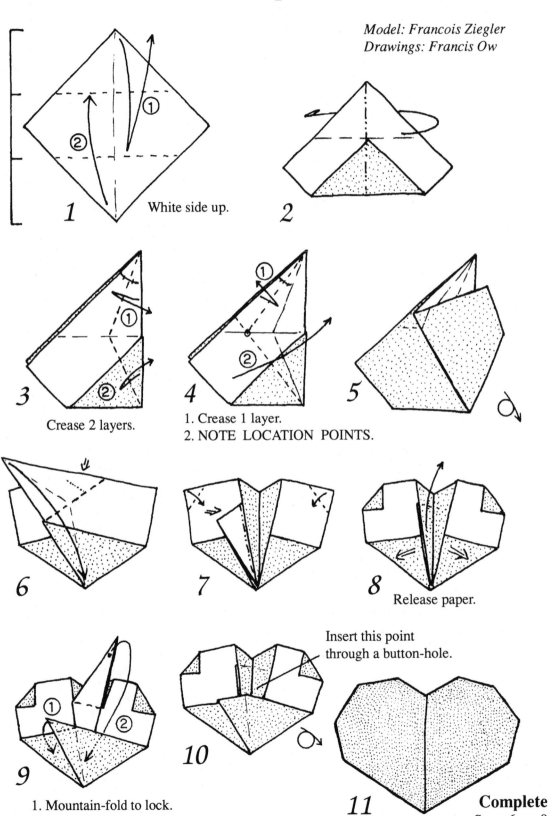

1 White side up.

2

3 Crease 2 layers.

4
1. Crease 1 layer.
2. NOTE LOCATION POINTS.

5

6

7

8 Release paper.

9
1. Mountain-fold to lock.
2. Insert point.

10

Insert this point through a button-hole.

11 **Complete**
See p.6, no.8

Winged Heart [Coeur Ailé]

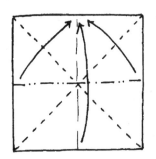

1 White side up.
Form Waterbomb base.

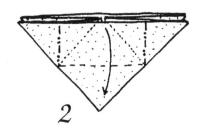

2

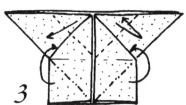

3

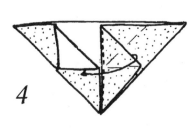

4

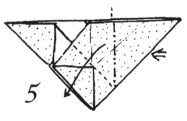

5 Squash.

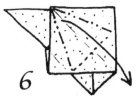

6 Petal-fold.

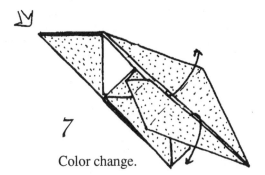

7 Color change.

8

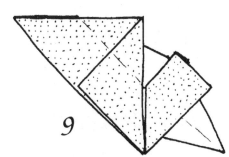

9 Repeat steps 4 to 8
for the left side.

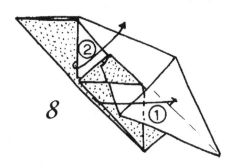

10

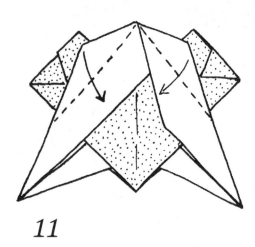

11

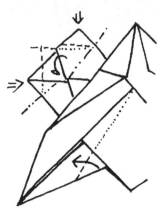

12 Repeat above folds for the right side.

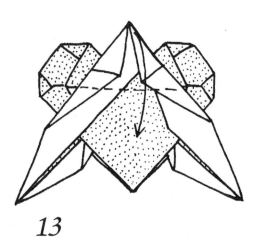

13

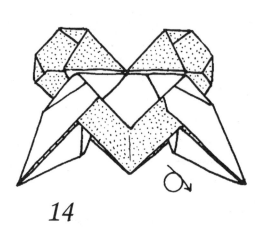

14

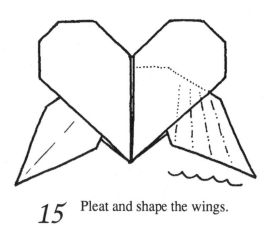

15 Pleat and shape the wings.

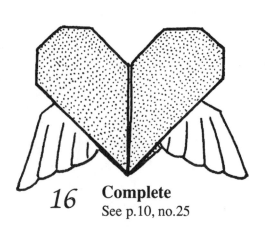

16 **Complete**
See p.10, no.25

Model: Francois Ziegler / Drawings: Francis Ow

Flying Heart

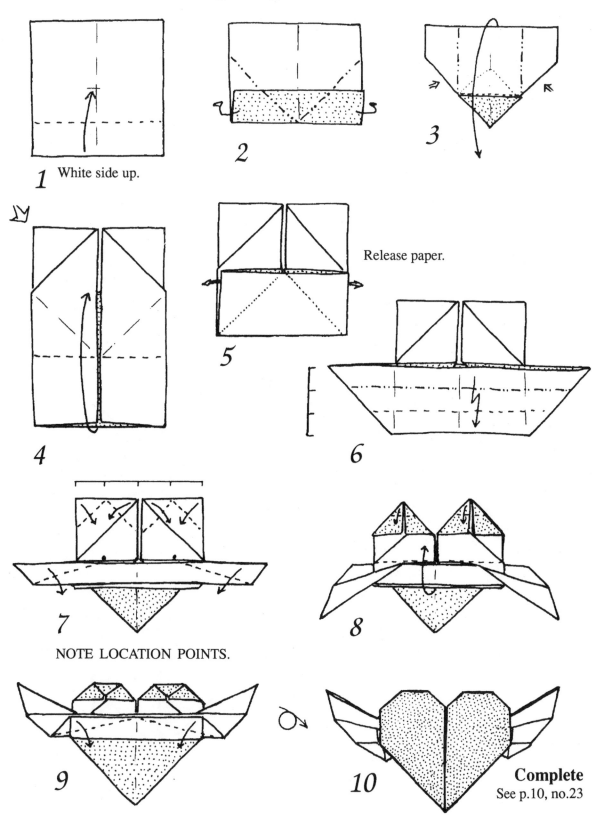

1 White side up.

2

3

4

5 Release paper.

6

7 NOTE LOCATION POINTS.

8

9

10

Complete
See p.10, no.23

Model: Paul Ee / Drawings: Francis Ow

A Heart for Two

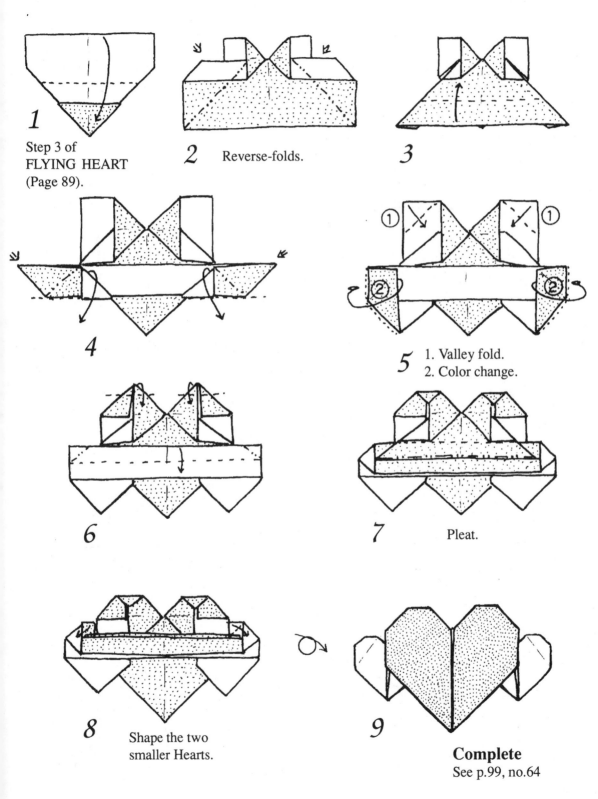

1 Step 3 of
FLYING HEART
(Page 89).

2 Reverse-folds.

3

4

5
1. Valley fold.
2. Color change.

6

7 Pleat.

8 Shape the two
smaller Hearts.

9
Complete
See p.99, no.64

Model: Paul Ee / Drawings: Francis Ow

90

Love Birds

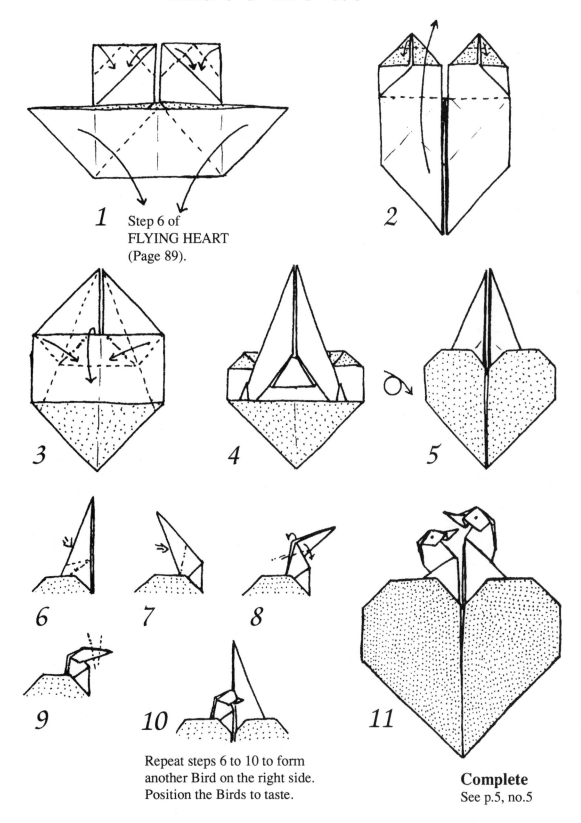

1 Step 6 of
FLYING HEART
(Page 89).

2

3

4

5

6

7

8

9

10

Repeat steps 6 to 10 to form
another Bird on the right side.
Position the Birds to taste.

11

Complete
See p.5, no.5

Model: Paul Ee / Drawings: Francis Ow

Love Dove

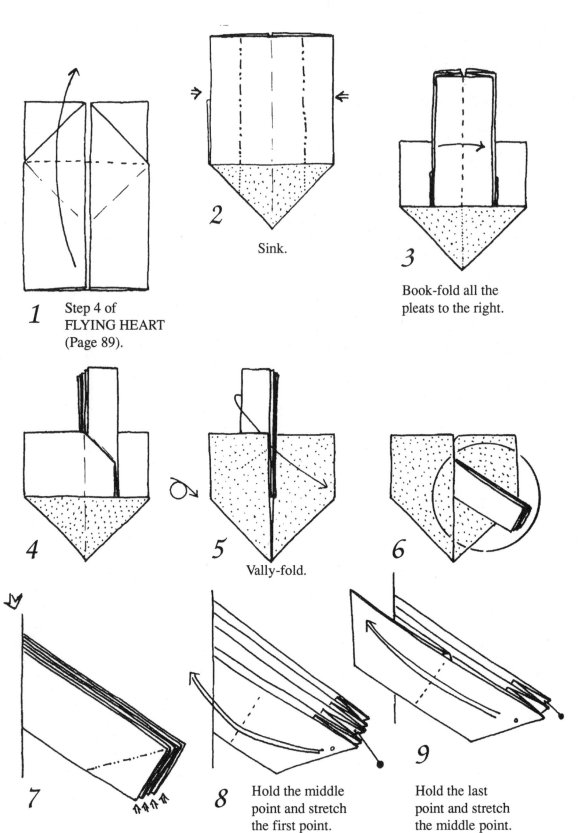

1 Step 4 of FLYING HEART (Page 89).

2 Sink.

3 Book-fold all the pleats to the right.

4

5 Vally-fold.

6

7

8 Hold the middle point and stretch the first point.

9 Hold the last point and stretch the middle point.

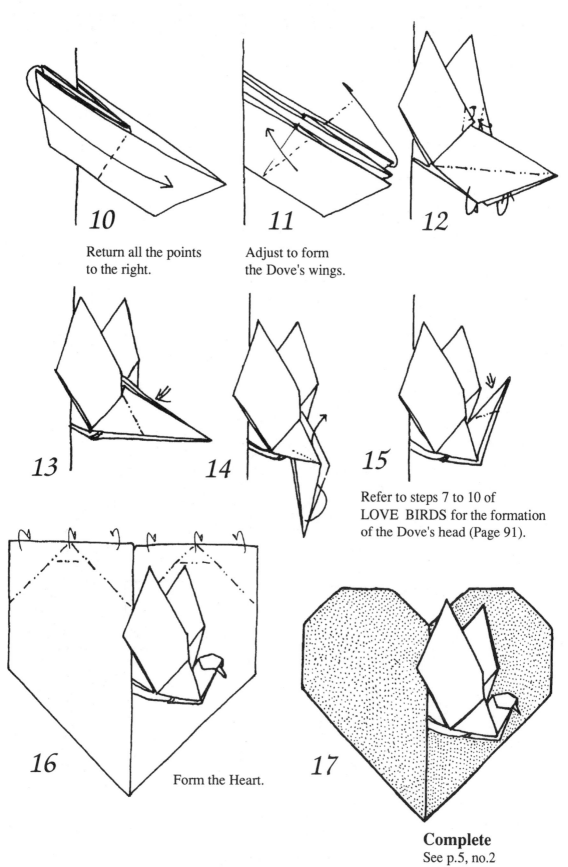

10

Return all the points
to the right.

11

Adjust to form
the Dove's wings.

12

13

14

15

Refer to steps 7 to 10 of
LOVE BIRDS for the formation
of the Dove's head (Page 91).

16

Form the Heart.

17

Complete
See p.5, no.2

Model: Paul Ee / Drawings: Francis Ow

Circle of Hearts [Modular]

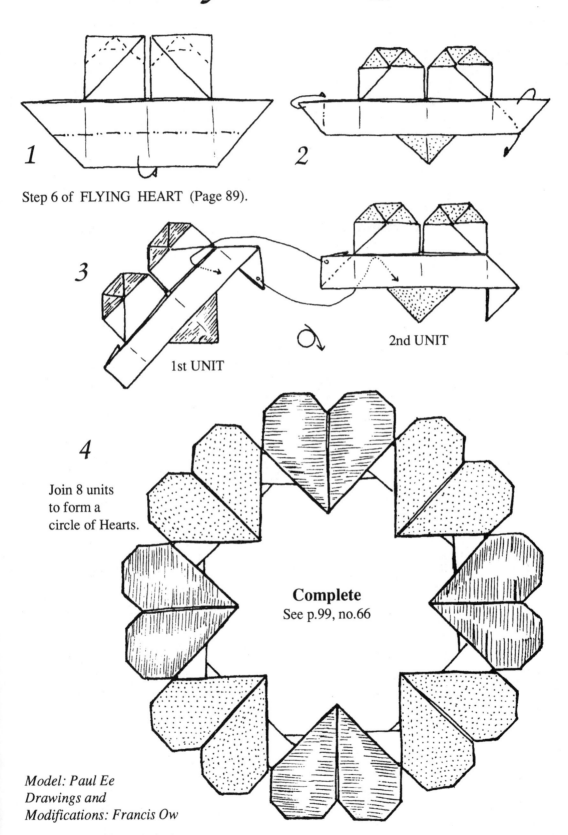

1

Step 6 of FLYING HEART (Page 89).

2

3

1st UNIT

2nd UNIT

4

Join 8 units
to form a
circle of Hearts.

Complete
See p.99, no.66

Model: Paul Ee
Drawings and
Modifications: Francis Ow

Heart Ring 3 / Book Marker

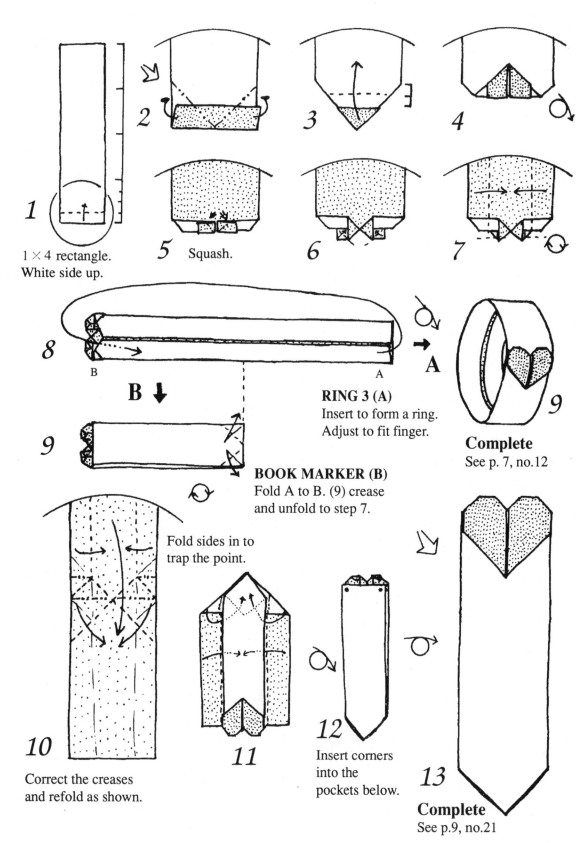

1

1 × 4 rectangle.
White side up.

2

3

4

5 Squash.

6

7

8

B

B ⬇

9

RING 3 (A)
Insert to form a ring.
Adjust to fit finger.

A

9

Complete
See p. 7, no.12

BOOK MARKER (B)
Fold A to B. (9) crease
and unfold to step 7.

10

Correct the creases
and refold as shown.

Fold sides in to
trap the point.

11

12

Insert corners
into the
pockets below.

13

Complete
See p.9, no.21

Heart Corner Marker

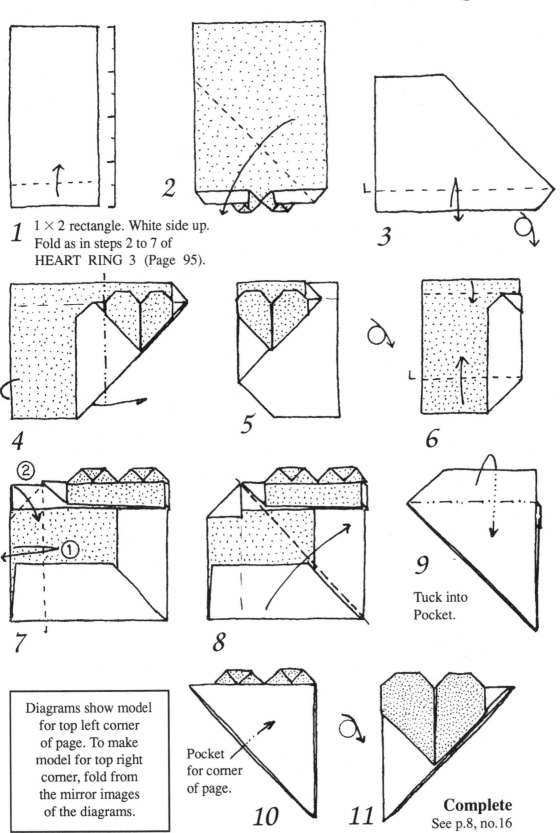

1 1 × 2 rectangle. White side up.
Fold as in steps 2 to 7 of
HEART RING 3 (Page 95).

2

3

4

5

6

7

8

9 Tuck into Pocket.

Diagrams show model for top left corner of page. To make model for top right corner, fold from the mirror images of the diagrams.

10 Pocket for corner of page.

11 **Complete**
See p.8, no.16

Heart Corner Marker 2

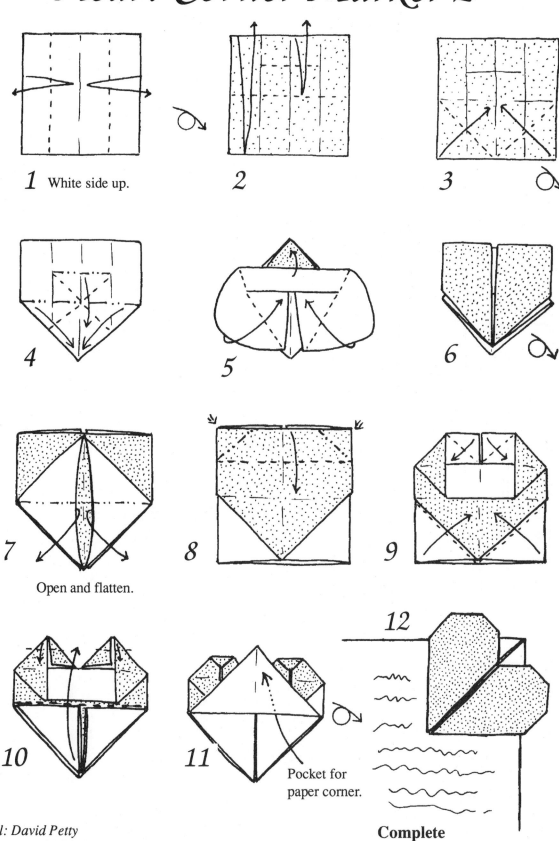

1 White side up.

2

3

4

5 Open and flatten.

6

7

8

9

10

11 Pocket for paper corner.

12

Model: David Petty
Drawings and Modifications: Francis Ow

Complete
See p.8, no.15

Twin Hearts with Stand

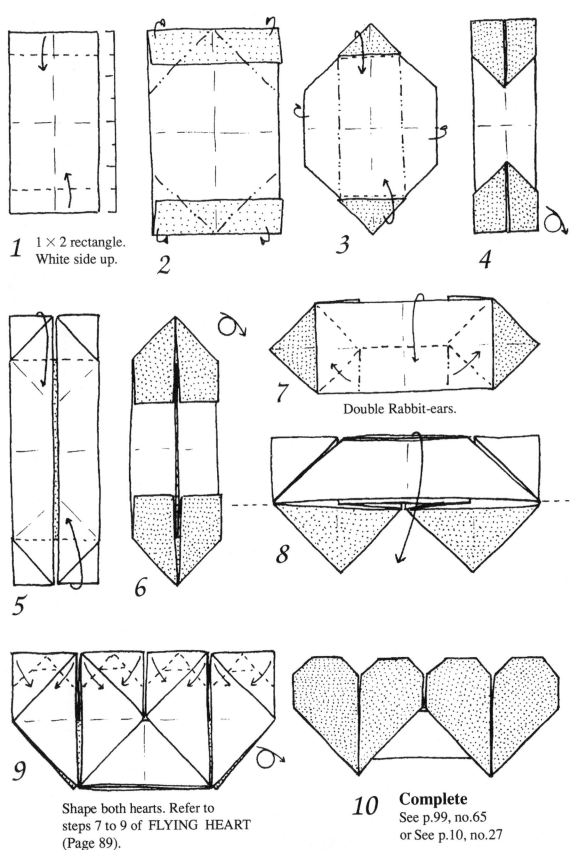

1 1 × 2 rectangle. White side up.

2

3

4

5

6

7 Double Rabbit-ears.

8

9 Shape both hearts. Refer to steps 7 to 9 of FLYING HEART (Page 89).

10 **Complete** See p.99, no.65 or See p.10, no.27

98

62

63

64

65

66

67

68

69

70

99

Changing Heart

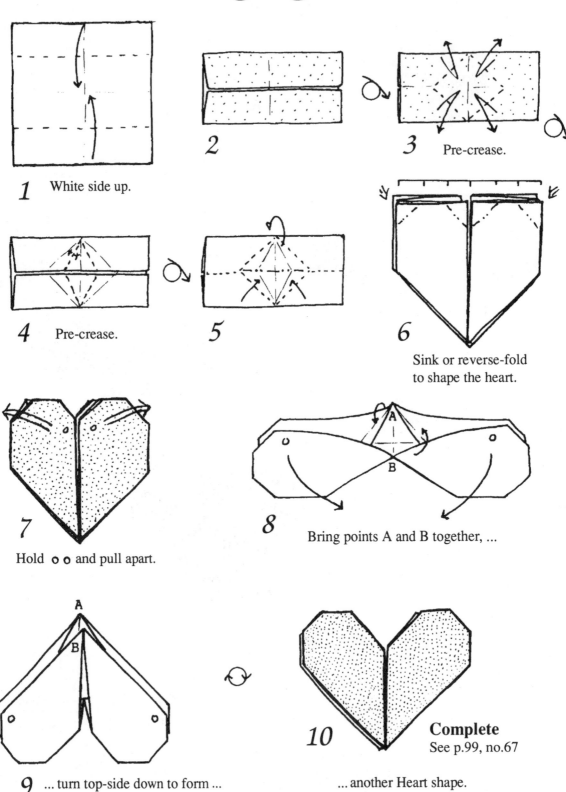

1 White side up.

2

3 Pre-crease.

4 Pre-crease.

5

6 Sink or reverse-fold to shape the heart.

7 Hold o o and pull apart.

8 Bring points A and B together, ...

9 ... turn top-side down to form ...

10 **Complete**
See p.99, no.67

... another Heart shape.

Model: Edwin Young / Drawings: Francis Ow

Heart Tangram

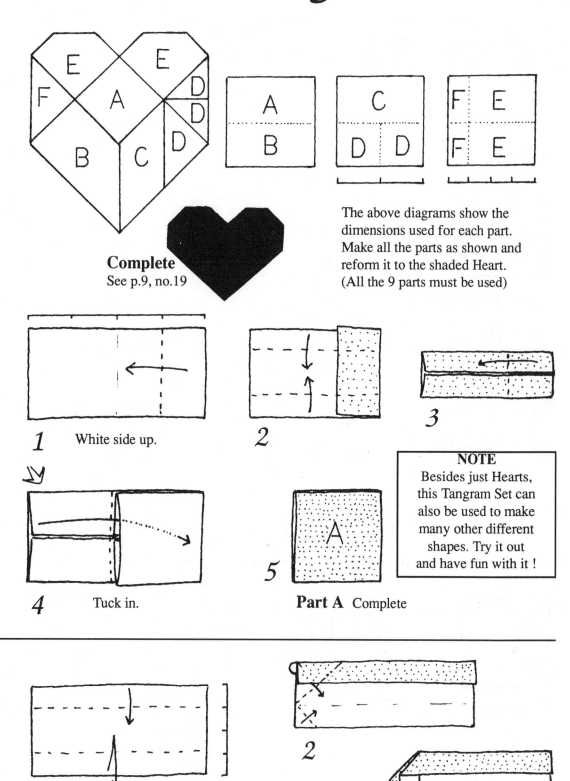

Complete
See p.9, no.19

The above diagrams show the dimensions used for each part. Make all the parts as shown and reform it to the shaded Heart. (All the 9 parts must be used)

1   White side up.

2

3

4   Tuck in.

5   **Part A** Complete

NOTE
Besides just Hearts, this Tangram Set can also be used to make many other different shapes. Try it out and have fun with it !

1   White side up.

2

3

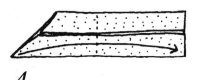

4

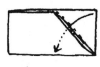

5 Tuck in.

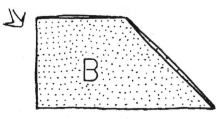

6 **Part B** Complete

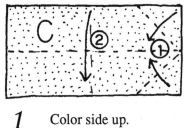

1 Color side up.

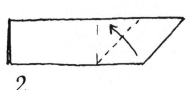

2

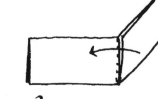

3

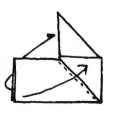

4 Color change.

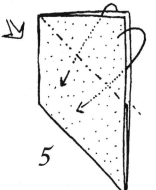

5 Tuck the 2 flaps into the pocket.

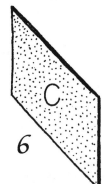

6 **Part C** Complete

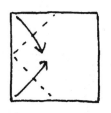

1 White side up.

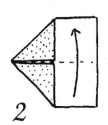

2

3

4 Tuck in.

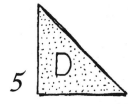

5 **Part D** Complete
Make one more.

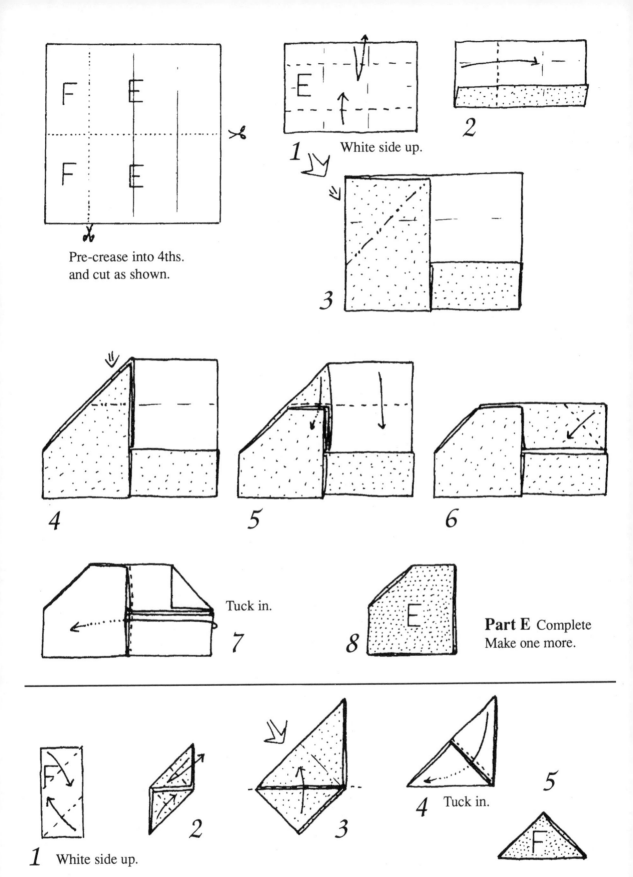

Pre-crease into 4ths.
and cut as shown.

1 White side up.

2

3

4

5

6

7 Tuck in.

8 **Part E** Complete
Make one more.

1 White side up.

2

3

4 Tuck in.

5

Part F Complete   Make one more.

Love is Blind

To make the model large enough to wear,
use a 50mm × 600 mm (2" × 23 1/2") rectangle.

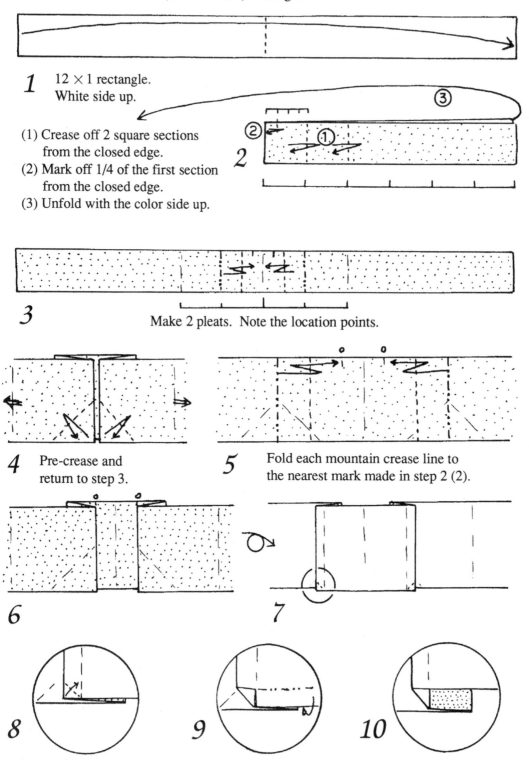

1 12 × 1 rectangle.
White side up.

(1) Crease off 2 square sections
from the closed edge.
(2) Mark off 1/4 of the first section
from the closed edge.
(3) Unfold with the color side up.

2

3 Make 2 pleats. Note the location points.

4 Pre-crease and
return to step 3.

5 Fold each mountain crease line to
the nearest mark made in step 2 (2).

6

7

8

9

10

SECTION ENLARGED. Repeat steps 8 to 10 for the right side.

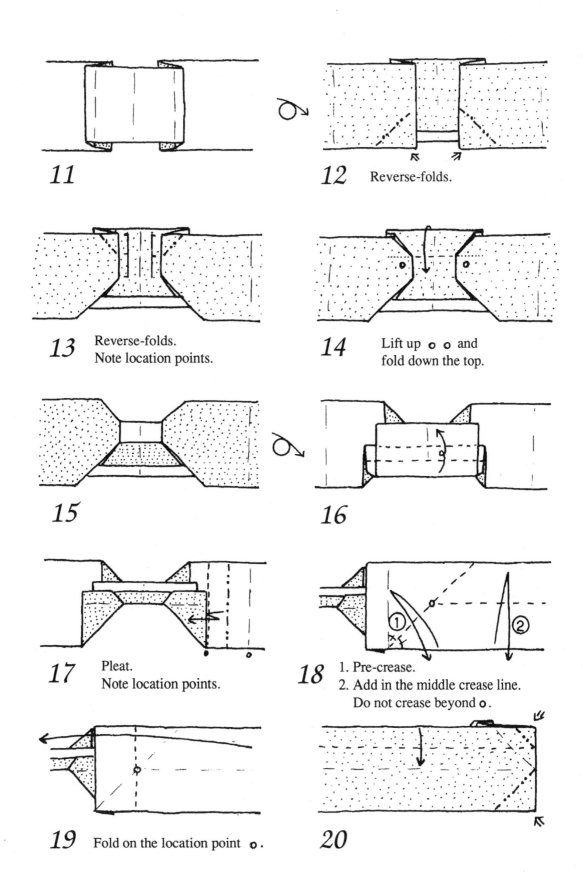

11

12 Reverse-folds.

13 Reverse-folds.
Note location points.

14 Lift up o o and
fold down the top.

15

16

17 Pleat.
Note location points.

18 1. Pre-crease.
2. Add in the middle crease line.
Do not crease beyond o.

19 Fold on the location point o.

20

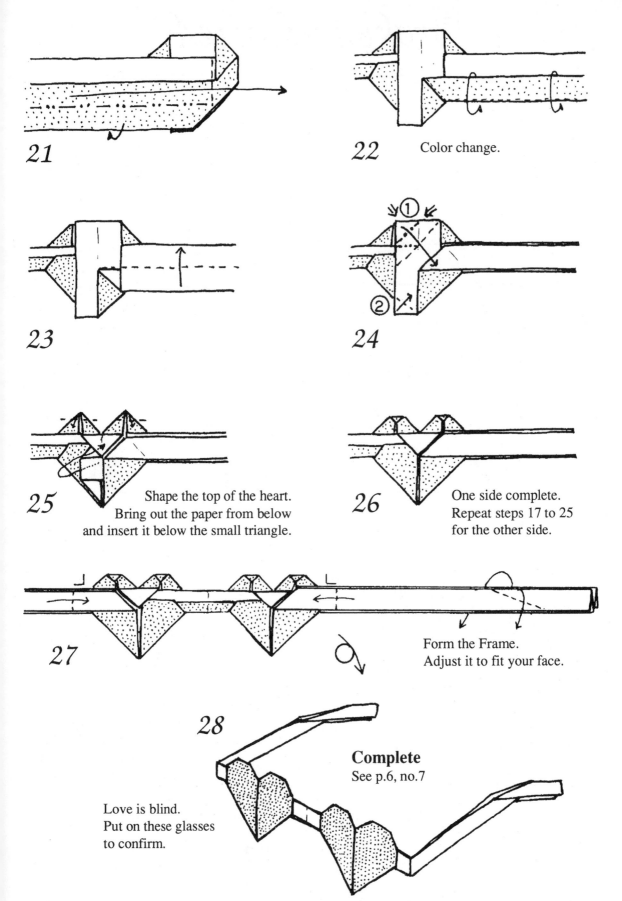

21

22 Color change.

23

24

25 Shape the top of the heart. Bring out the paper from below and insert it below the small triangle.

26 One side complete. Repeat steps 17 to 25 for the other side.

27 Form the Frame. Adjust it to fit your face.

28

Complete
See p.6, no.7

Love is blind.
Put on these glasses
to confirm.

Broken Hearted

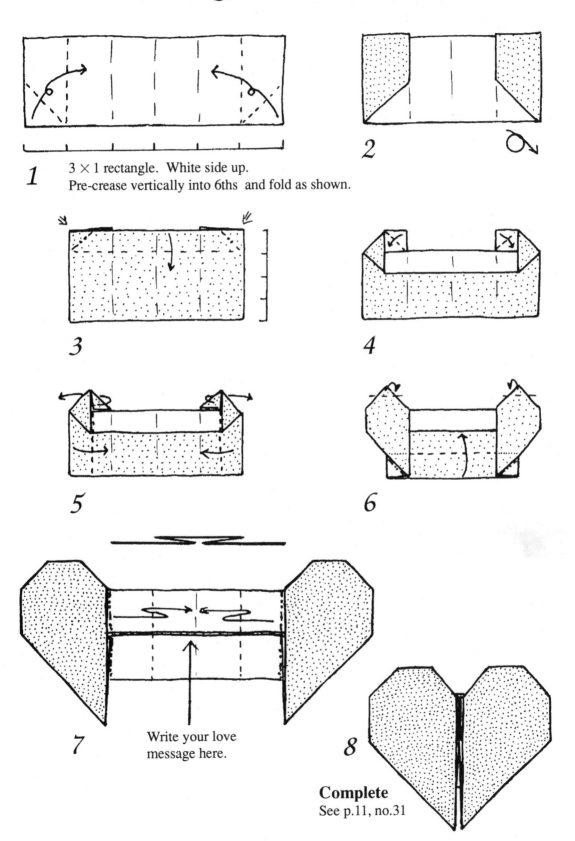

1   3 × 1 rectangle. White side up.
Pre-crease vertically into 6ths and fold as shown.

2

3

4

5

6

7   Write your love
message here.

8   **Complete**
See p.11, no.31

107

3-D Heart (Corrie's)

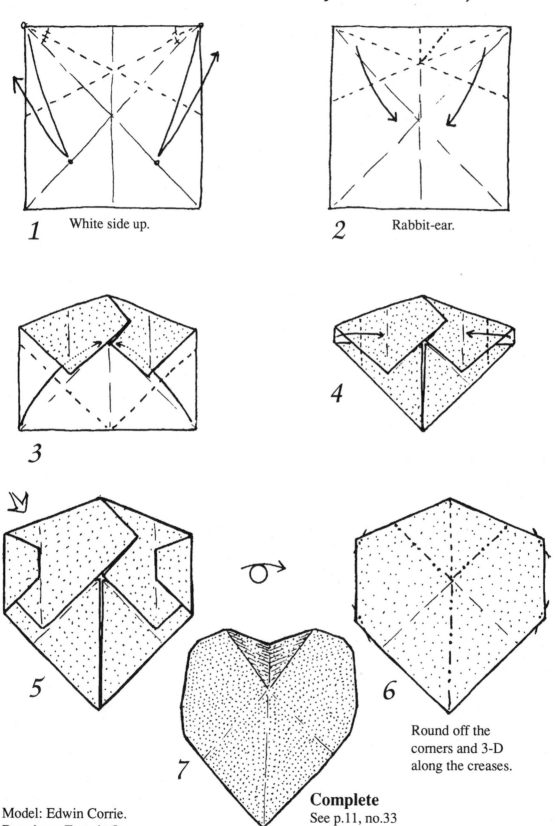

1 White side up.

2 Rabbit-ear.

3

4

5

6 Round off the corners and 3-D along the creases.

7 **Complete**
See p.11, no.33

Model: Edwin Corrie.
Drawings: Francis Ow.

Heart 2

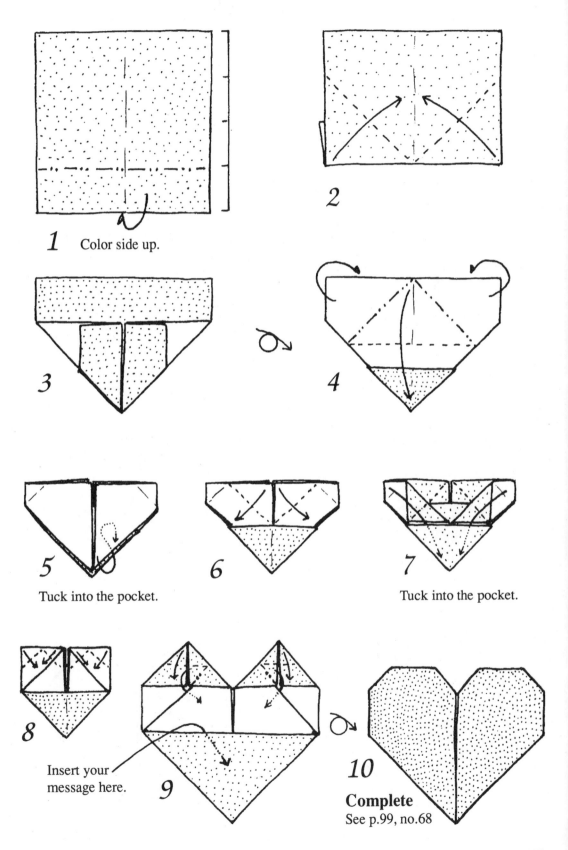

1   Color side up.

2

3

4

5

Tuck into the pocket.

6

7

Tuck into the pocket.

8

Insert your
message here.

9

10

Complete
See p.99, no.68

Heart 3

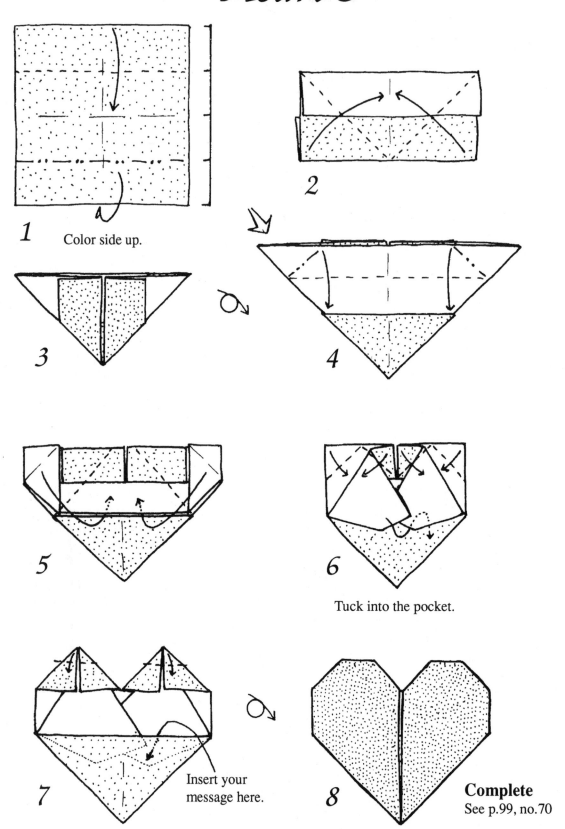

1 Color side up.

2

3

4

5

6 Tuck into the pocket.

7 Insert your message here.

8 **Complete**
See p.99, no.70

Model: Edwin Corrie / Drawings: Francis Ow

House of Love

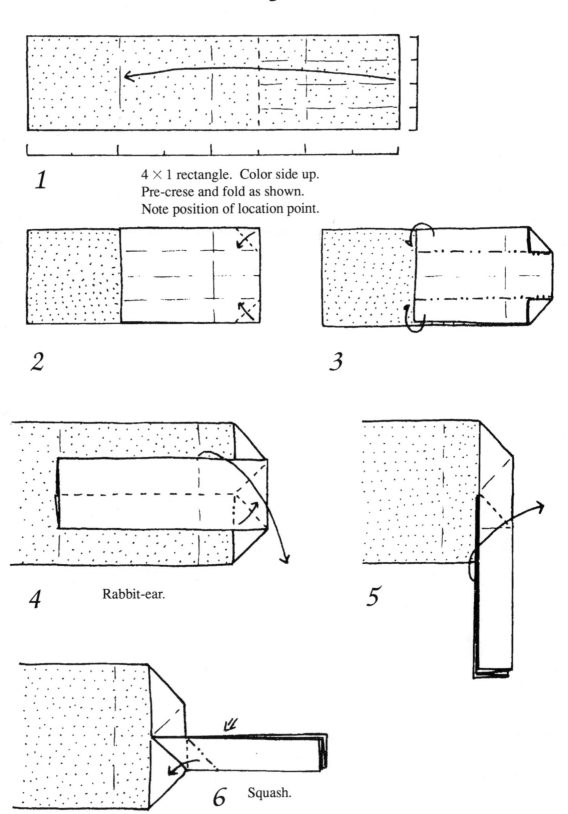

1 4 × 1 rectangle. Color side up.
Pre-crese and fold as shown.
Note position of location point.

2

3

4 Rabbit-ear.

5

6 Squash.

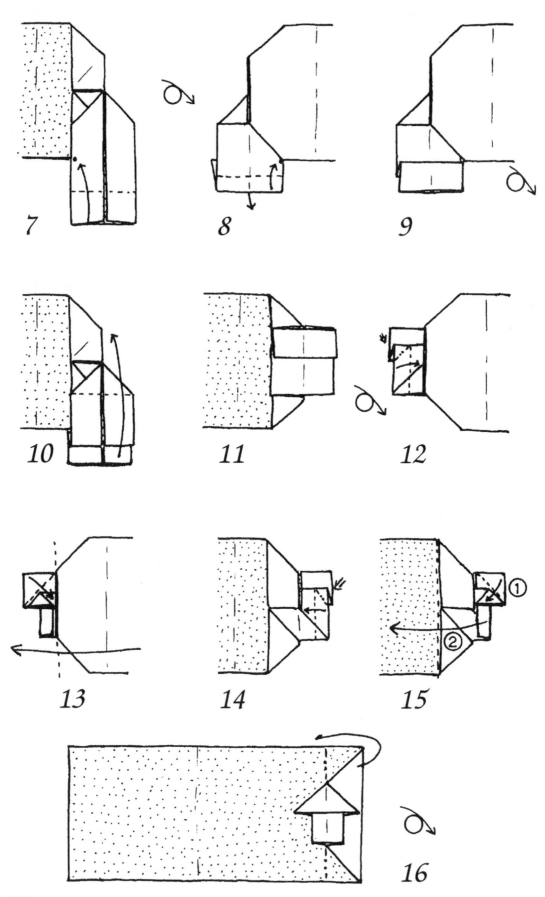

7

8

9

10

11

12

13

14

15

16

112

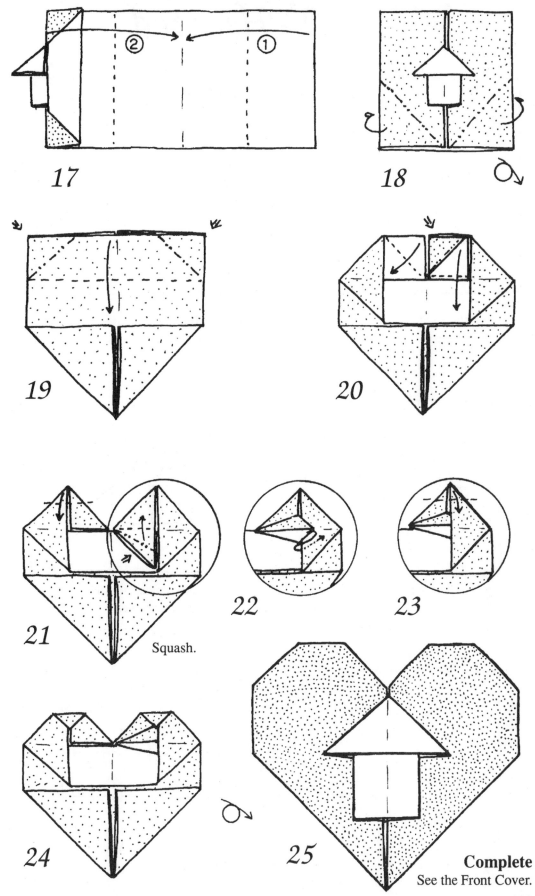

17

18

19

20

21

Squash.

22

23

24

25

Complete
See the Front Cover.

"O"-Hearted

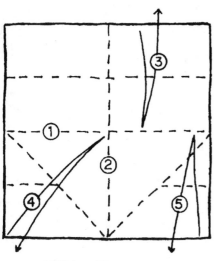

1 White side up.
Pre-crease accordingly.

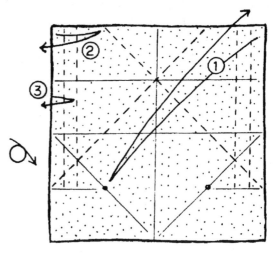

2 Add in the creases
accordingly.

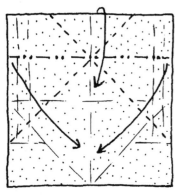

3 Off-set
Waterbomb Base.

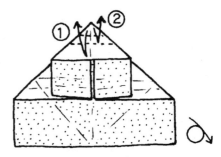

4 Pre-crease, unfold
and turn over.

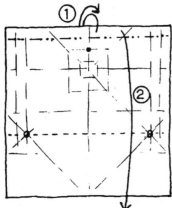

5 1. Pre-crease.
2. Fold down (note location).

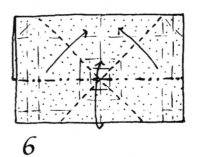

6

Refold the off-set Waterbomb
Base on the top layer only.

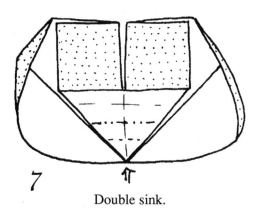

7

Double sink.

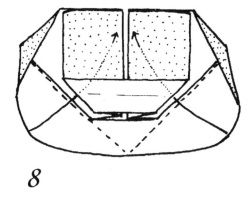

8

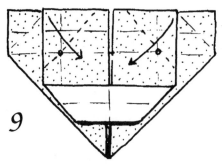

9

Note the location points.

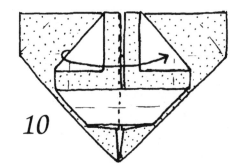

10

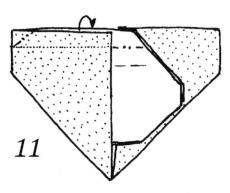

11

Mountain-fold
the bottom layer.

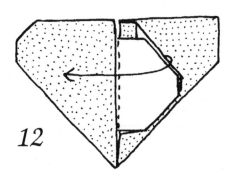

12

Fold the 2 flaps to the left,
repeat step 11 and
return 1 flap to the right.

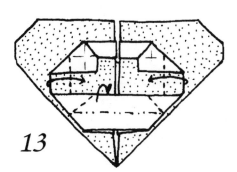

13

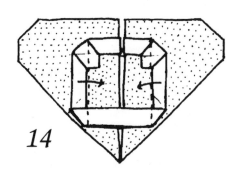

14

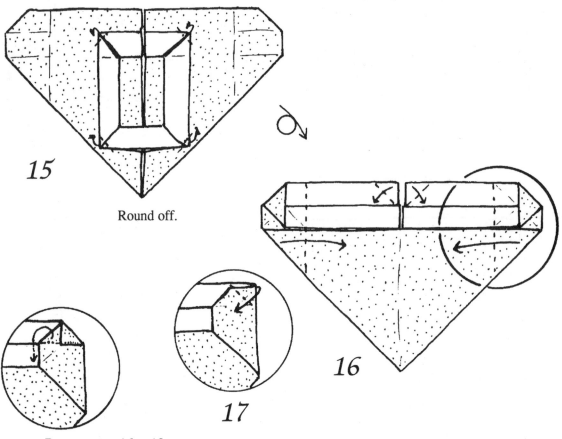

15

Round off.

16

17

18 Repeat steps 16 to 18 for the left side.

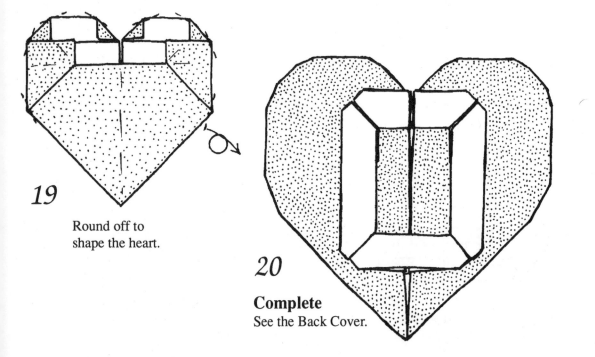

19

Round off to shape the heart.

20

Complete
See the Back Cover.

Heart 4

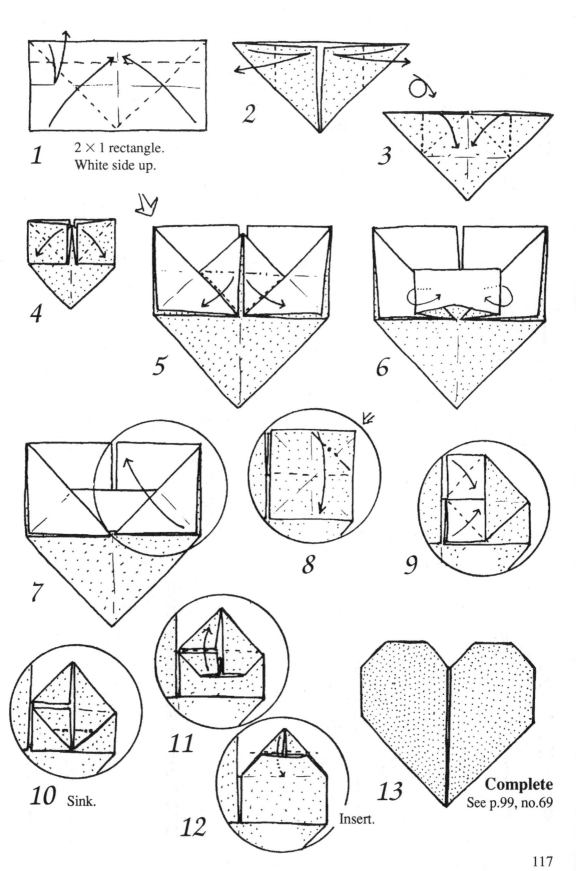

1   2 × 1 rectangle.
White side up.

2

3

4

5

6

7

8

9

10   Sink.

11

12   Insert.

13   **Complete**
See p.99, no.69

2-Piece Heart Coaster

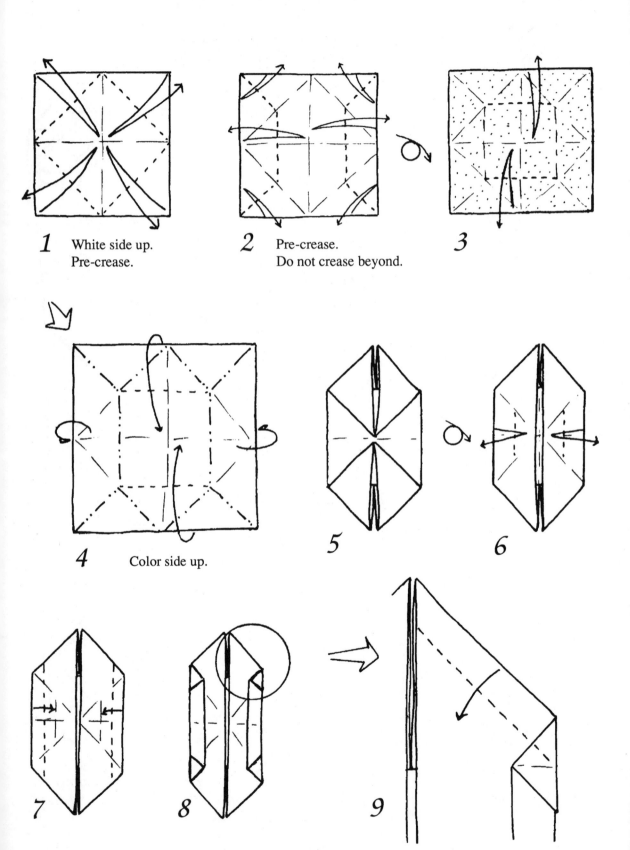

1 White side up.
Pre-crease.

2 Pre-crease.
Do not crease beyond.

3

4 Color side up.

5

6

7

8

9